Czech and Slovak Railways

Three Decades of Change, 1990–2020s

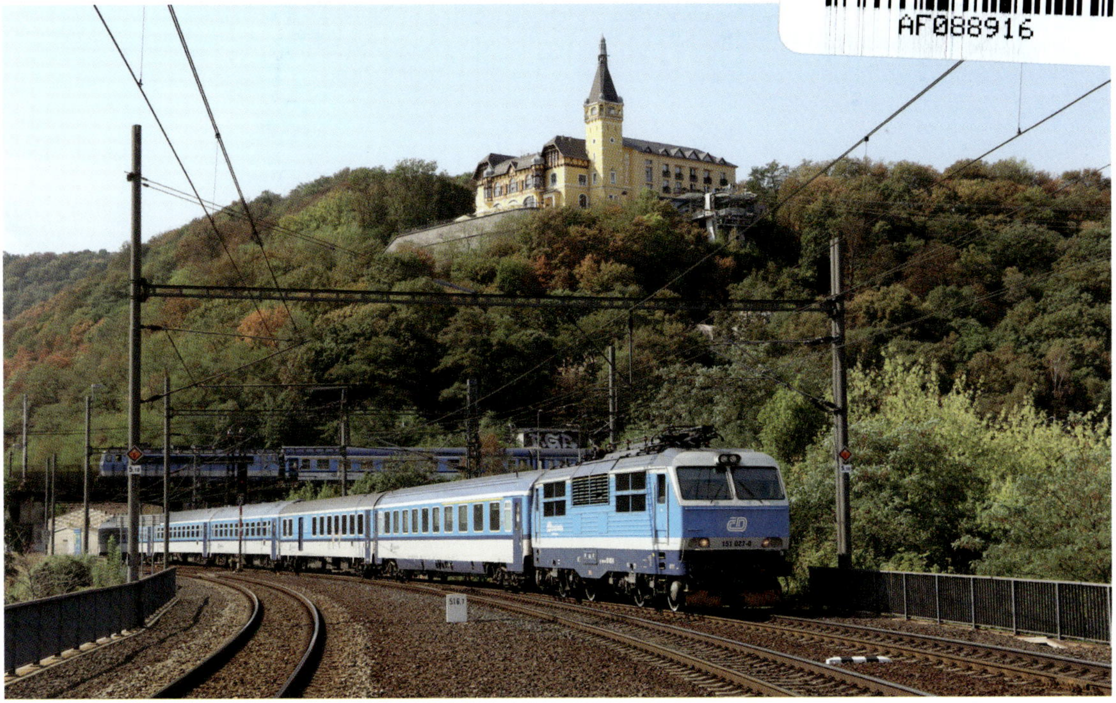

KEITH FENDER

KEY Books

WORLD RAILWAYS SERIES, VOLUME 2

Front cover image: Slovak Railways (ZSSK) loco 361 125-8 at Prague's main Praha hl.n station on arrival with fast train Ex220 from Žilina on 11 April 2017. The loco, originally built in what is now the Czech Republic, has been fully modernised, along with 21 similar examples, for 160km/h operation in both parts of the former Czechoslovakia.

Back cover image: A remarkable variety of freight locos and operators can be seen in the Czech Republic and Slovakia. In this view at Ostrava Svinov on 14 June 2016, a pair of modernised Class 753.7 locos 753 738 + 753 729 head south with a loaded coal train, passing veteran Škoda-built electric 182 041-4, used by Czech operator IDS, but leased from privatized Slovak rail maintenance firm ŽOS Zvolen.

Title page image: Czech state-owned operator, České dráhy (ČD), has re-liveried almost all its fleet in this smart blue and white livery in the last decade. ČD is now starting to replace much of its fleet dating from the 1970s and 1980s, such as Class 151 locos like 151 027-0, which is seen arriving at Usti nad Labem from Prague on 19 August 2018. Rebuilt for 160km/h operation in the 1990s, it will probably soon be withdrawn and replaced by new modern locos. Passing above the train is a regional service from another station in the city to Kolín; these services will be in the hands of private operator Regiojet from 2022, as ČD has lost the contract to run them.

Contents page image: Czech and Slovak locos meet at Břeclav, close to the border between both countries and neighbouring Austria on 10 August 2015. On the left is Slovak Railways (ZSSK) 'Gorilla' 350 005-5, with a train from Prague to Budapest, while arriving alongside is more modern Czech Railways (ČD) loco 380 011-7. with a train from Warsaw to Vienna.

Published by Key Books
An imprint of Key Publishing Ltd
PO Box 100
Stamford
Lincs PE19 1XQ

www.keypublishing.com

The right of Keith Fender to be identified as the author of this book has been asserted in accordance with the Copyright, Designs and Patents Act 1988 Sections 77 and 78.

Copyright © Keith Fender, 2021

ISBN 978 1 80282 029 4

All rights reserved. Reproduction in whole or in part in any form whatsoever or by any means is strictly prohibited without the prior permission of the Publisher.

Typeset by SJmagic DESIGN SERVICES, India.

Thanks and acknowledgements
Thanks are due to multiple companies and individuals for their assistance over the years and with information and illustrations for this book, especially České dráhy, Regiojet, ZSSK, Správa železnic, Škoda Transportation, Siemens, Bombardier, and Leo Express. All pictures are by the author except where shown. My thanks to Shaun Wallace for his help with several pictures and special thanks to Sue for all her help.

References
The UK magazines *Modern Railways* and *Today's Railways Europe* have both offered good coverage in English of Czech and Slovak railway operations during the last three decades.

Large amounts of public source information from ZSSK, ŽSR, Správa železnic, Siemens, Bombardier, the Slovak national statistical service, and the European Commission have also been used to prepare this book.

The Slovak rail infrastructure manager ŽSR has a detailed online history of Slovakia's railways, available at www.zsr.sk/o-nas/historia-zeleznic in Slovak but web browsers will translate.

For detailed fleet information in English, *Czech and Slovak Railways* by Robert Pritchard, published by Platform 5 Publishing, is highly recommended.

For a detailed Czech and Slovak railway atlas, one is produced as part of the European railway atlas series, see https://europeanrailwayatlas.com. Alternatively, the free online 'openrailwaymap' site is an excellent resource www.openrailwaymap.org.

Contents

Chapter 1 Czechoslovakia and its railways: a historical introduction 4
Chapter 2 Railways in transition: 1989–93 16
Chapter 3 Two countries – two railways: 1993–2003 29
Chapter 4 EU membership and fleet development 41
Chapter 5 Central European rail freight hub 50
Chapter 6 Competition flourishes 57
Chapter 7 International connections enhanced 69
Chapter 8 Narrow gauge mixed fortunes 77
Chapter 9 Rail preservation large and small 87
Chapter 10 High speed future 92
Glossary 96

Chapter 1

Czechoslovakia and its railways: a historical introduction

Since 1993, the central European countries of the Czech Republic (also known officially in English as Czechia) and Slovakia have been the successors to the former Czechoslovakia, which had only existed as an independent country since 1918. Unlike many European countries, a glance at the railway map of what are now the two countries before World War One shows that much of the rail network not only still exists today, but has, in places, been expanded. Both countries were then in the northern part of the Austro-Hungarian Empire, ruled by the Hapsburg family since the 16th century, which in 1914 included all of modern-day Austria and Hungary and stretched from the western border with Switzerland, south to Dubrovnik in Croatia, and to modern day Kraków (Poland) and Lviv (Ukraine) in the north and east.

The Austro-Hungarian rail network was run by multiple companies; the pre-World War One map shows more than 40 major ones, although large state-owned Austrian and Hungarian operators had a significant role. The first railway line in what became Czechoslovakia was the Kaiser Ferdinands-Nordbahn (KFNB), designed to link Vienna and Kraków (then in the Austrian province of Galicia, now in Poland). This line opened to Břeclav (Lundenberg in German) on 7 July 1839, as did the branch northwest to Brno (then called Brünn) using locomotives built as kits by George Stephenson in Newcastle, England. Not just locos were imported from the UK; the KFNB also used left-hand running and this applied into the 21st century, only ending between Břeclav and Bohumín in December 2012.

The first railway in Slovakia opened nearly a decade later and connected Marchegg, then, as now, on the Austrian border, with Bratislava. The first train ran on 20 August 1848, using a connecting line from the KFNB route at Gänserndorf to Marchegg. Over the next few years, the new line was then extended in stages east to Budapest via Štúrovo.

By World War One, the Austrian-run network in what is now the Czech Republic had seen investment. Brand new electrified lines using direct current systems had been built by private companies between

The main station in Plzeň (in German, Pilsen, and the birthplace of Pilsner beer) is the Art Nouveau Plzeň hlavní nádraží, which dates from the last days of the Austro-Hungarian Empire. Seen here, on 30 January 2012, is ČD diesel loco 754 060-2 and a local train to Domažlice, which has since been replaced by modern DMUs. Finished in 1907, the dome was made at the nearby Škoda factory and then rebuilt in the 1950s after extensive damage from Allied air raids in April 1945. The station has been carefully renovated in the last few years with modern facilities, such as lifts and escalators as well.

Private investors built railways in the years prior to World War One. The first purpose built electric railway in central Europe opened in 1903 between Tabor and Bechyně, using vehicles built by Ringhoffer in Prague. The first such vehicle is still in use for weekend heritage services; M400 001 seen leaving Tabor with the 10.00 service to Bechyně on 10 July 2004. The line originally used a three wire 2x700V DC electrification system; this was converted to 1500V DC in 1938 and will be converted again in 2023–24 to 25kV AC, removing the ability to operate the original train.

Tabor and Bechyně (opening in June 1903 and now electrified at 1500V DC) and Rybník to Lipno nad Vltavou (opened in December 1911 using 1280V DC electrification). Monumental new Art Nouveau stations had also been built in Prague, Plzeň and Brno during the first decade of the 20th century.

Independence

To understand how the rail network developed from the early 20th century to the present day, we need to understand a little of the history of Czechoslovakia. The independent Czechoslovak state was declared in late October 1918, before World War One had ended. Following military defeat in northern Italy, Austria-Hungary sought an armistice with the 'Entente' Allied powers on 3 November 1918, a week before Germany followed suit. The Hapsburg Empire then fragmented into a wide variety of nation states, some very short lived as the victorious Allies were determined to redraw the map of Europe. In the peace treaties negotiated in Paris in 1919, the new Czechoslovakia, plus other new or newly independent central European countries, was created, mainly by dismantling the old German and Austro-Hungarian empires, which had ruled some of the territory for centuries.

Czech politician Tomáš Masaryk had emerged as the main proponent of Czechoslovak independence from Austria-Hungary during the war and crucially had met with US President Woodrow Wilson to promote the cause. At the Paris peace conference, Wilson supported 'self-determination' for the new nations of central Europe, and the new Czechoslovakia comprised the majority of the territory inhabited by Czech and Slovak speaking people, but also included substantial minorities of people who spoke the languages of the former imperial powers. In the west of the new country, especially in the Sudetenland border region, there were millions of ethnic German speakers as the Czech regions of Bohemia and Moravia were located near Austria and Germany. In the east, in what is now largely Slovakia, there were large numbers of Hungarian speakers as, pre-1918, all of modern-day Slovakia was administered as part of Hungary.

In recognition of their role in achieving independence, both Tomáš Masaryk and Woodrow Wilson had major stations named after them in Prague; the former Austrian state railway Praha státní nádraží / Prag Staatsbahnhof terminus was renamed Praha Masarykovo nádraží in 1919, and since 1990 has had the name again, having lost it several times under Nazi and communist regimes in between. Prague's main station was renamed after President Wilson in 1919 as Praha Wilsonovo nádraží, a name it retained until World War Two and briefly again afterwards; today the station is simply Praha Hlavní nádraží (Prague main station). Until 1918, it was known as Kaiser-Franz-Joseph-Bahnhof / Nádraží císaře Františka Josefa.

New country – new national railway

The creation of the new Czechoslovakia impacted the rail network and, in some cases, such as around Břeclav, the borders were literally drawn to ensure railway lines remained inside the new country, and not in neighbouring Austria. As a result of this policy, a small part of former German eastern Silesia, around what is now the Czech town of Hlucin, was incorporated in the new Czechoslovakia; the rest of eastern Silesia became part of the newly independent Poland. Incorporation of parts of the east of the new country was delayed by a short-lived invasion of Slovakia by Hungarian forces, which were briefly under the control of a communist government in Budapest; by June 1919, Czechoslovakia had taken control of its eastern borders.

In 2021, the line from Opava to Hlucin remained one of the few where ČD operates trains of DMU trailers hauled by locomotives at busy times. 742 449-2 is seen at Hlucin on 19 April 2006, on arrival from Opava východ; Class 714 locos replaced Class 742s around 2010 on these duties. Hlucin illustrates the complex history of the area and its railways. The railway from Opava only reached Hlucin (formerly Hultschin) in 1913, and the line and the town were transferred to the new Czechoslovakia from Germany in 1920, after a local referendum chose this. ČSD extended the line to Petřkovice, near Ostrava, but plans to extend it to the Polish border were never realised. The extension to the line was short lived as, in 1950–52, the Hlucin to Petřkovice line was converted to be part of the Ostrava tram system, although it was shut in 1982 and has since been rebuilt as a road.

The new country created a state railway, Československé státní dráhy (ČSD – Czechoslovak State Railways), that was part of the Transport Ministry in Prague and took over the rail network and the existing rolling stock, this coming largely from the previous Austrian and Hungarian state-owned operators, plus multiple privately owned 'local railways', which were nationalised over a period of two decades. The new ČSD based in Prague was not initially universally popular with some existing railway employees; they were given three years to learn Czech or Slovak if they did not speak it already, as these languages replaced German and Hungarian as the official operating languages.

Much of the industrial capacity of the former Austro-Hungarian Empire had been located in Bohemia and Moravia with heavy engineering, including railway equipment, made in Plzeň and Prague. Coal mining and iron/steel production was concentrated in Moravia, around Ostrava. The new ČSD inherited a very densely built rail network in Bohemia, which represented half of the entire new national network in terms of length and 43 per cent of the traffic. In the east of the new country, the rail network in Slovakia and the Ruthenia region in the extreme southeast (now part of Ukraine) represented just under a third of the network length but accounted for only 10 per cent of the traffic.

In the two decades of independent existence between 1918 and 1938, Czechoslovakia modernised its rail network, adding new lines to connect existing ones that previously were designed to serve cities that were now in different countries. The large fleet of mainly Austrian-built steam locos was rationalised and modernised or replaced with new locos. Czech-designed and -built steam locomotives from the Škoda works in Plzeň, both for ČSD and export internationally, were regarded as modern and as advanced as those from leading Western European builders.

ČSD was an early adopter of diesel power for passenger trains, introducing over 100 petrol or diesel powered two-axle railcars between 1927 and 1938 for regional services to replace steam. Two stylish streamlined diesel-powered 130km/h bogie rail cars named 'Slovak Arrow' (Slovenská strela) for Prague to Bratislava services were introduced in 1936 and built by Tatra. Plans for further express railcars known as 'Silver Arrow' (Stříbrný šíp) were disrupted by the German invasion and only a prototype was built. All the ČSD diesel passenger trains were taken out of service once World War Two began, owing to fuel shortages.

ČSD also took the first steps to main line electrification with electrification at 1500V DC of some suburban lines in Prague from 1928, using five Škoda-built Class E466.0 (later E467.0) electric locos, these incorporating contemporary Swiss electrical equipment. The aim of this electrification is recognisable to 21st century readers, to reduce pollution in Prague by replacing steam locomotive use.

On 14 March 1939, ČSD presented its new 130km/h Stříbrný šíp ('Silver Arrow') railcar built by ČKD, which had been under development since 1936 and incorporated what was then highly innovative aluminium and steel construction. Unfortunately, the next day Prague was occupied by the German army and the Stříbrný šíp was not used until 1948. After only five years in service, it was stored in 1952, but survived to be restored back to working order by ČD between 2011 and 2016 and is seen in this picture at its public re-presentation in Ostrava in 2016. The sole surviving 'Slovak Arrow' (Slovenská strela) railcar has also been restored to working order in recent years, after some time as a museum exhibit, making its first test runs on the national network in late 2020. (České dráhy)

Břeclav station was the first to open in what became Czechoslovakia, initially served by steam locos built by George Stephenson in England. After Czechoslovakia gained independence in 1918, reconstruction of the line connecting Břeclav with Bratislava, by building a double-track line from Devínska Nová Ves to Břeclav, was a national priority, enabling frequent express trains between Prague and Bratislava and removing the need for trains to reverse in Břeclav. The rebuilt line opened fully on 11 November 1929. Škoda-built electric loco 242 253-3 is seen at Břeclav on 23 November 2019.

A far away country

The geo-political developments in central Europe in the mid-1930s, with the rise to power of the Nazi Party under Adolf Hitler in neighbouring Germany, led to the end of the original Czechoslovak state. In March 1938, German troops occupied Austria and it became part of the German state and, in the process, the west of Czechoslovakia was surrounded by German forces. In anticipation of such a threat, Czechoslovakia had concluded a defence treaty with France in 1924 and built a series of fortifications based on the French Maginot Line, around the western border of the Sudetenland region of Bohemia.

Just as the Maginot Line proved to be an ineffective deterrent or defence from invasion for France in 1940, the Czech fortifications were also largely useless, as the sizeable German-speaking minority in the region became the conduit for annexation instead. They had long been the target of Nazi propaganda and a substantial minority joined a Nazi-supporting party advocating the break-up of the country and integration into Germany.

After attempts by German forces to occupy territory by force, and multiple terrorist attacks by Nazi sympathisers, a series of international crisis meetings followed, and led to the British and French governments agreeing to German occupation of the Sudetenland at a conference held in Munich in September 1938, with Hungary awarded parts of eastern Slovakia and all of Ruthenia at the same time. This led to ČSD losing nearly a third of its network in the eastern part of the country, with large amounts of rolling stock incorporated into Hungarian operator MAV, while in the west, hundreds of locomotives were requisitioned by Germany.

Czechoslovakia and its railways: a historical introduction

The British Prime Minister, Neville Chamberlain, infamously referred to Czechoslovakia and the dispute with its German minority on British national radio on 27 September 1938 as a "quarrel in a far away country, between people of whom we know nothing" before flying from London to Munich to meet Hitler. When he returned from Munich three days later, he promised 'peace in our time', naively (along with much of public opinion in the UK and France at the time) expecting Hitler to comply with the agreement, thus preventing a new war in Europe. However, six months later in mid-March 1939, Germany invaded the rest of Bohemia and Moravia and ensured that Slovakia declared independence, with a fascist government taking power there that was closely aligned to Nazi Germany.

By the end of 1939, World War Two was underway following Germany's invasion of Poland; itself made easier by occupying Czechoslovakia, as German troops could invade Poland from the south. From 1939 and during World War Two, the German-administered Protectorate of Bohemia and Moravia was run for the benefit of Germany; its factories building weapons and equipment including steam locos. Non-German Czech residents were treated as second-class citizens, denied education or food rations compared to Germans, while the once thriving Jewish community was almost destroyed as part of the Holocaust.

By 1945, liberation beckoned; a resistance movement in Slovakia had been largely defeated in 1944, after open revolt by part of the Slovak army. Some of those fighting the Germans used armoured trains built secretly in railway workshops. Heavy fighting between the German and Soviet armies led to widespread damage in Slovakia, and parts of Moravia, especially around Ostrava, although Bohemia in the west saw less damage as Allied aircraft were unable to reach the area until 1944 and, despite some bombing of industrial sites, Prague emerged almost unscathed from World War Two.

Three armoured trains were built in September–October 1944 in Zvolen and were used in fighting with the German army as part of the Slovak National Uprising. One is preserved at the Uprising Museum in Banská Bystrica. Another, this time a replica built for a 1974 film and complete with a 2-8-2T steam loco, is plinthed in Zvolen under the castle and near the main station. Seen on 10 September 2005, the replica uses Soviet T34 tank turrets, although older Škoda-built LT-35 tanks were used on the originals.

American forces occupied Plzeň on 6 May 1945 and US Army reconnaissance units reached Prague in the last days of the war, where resistance fighters had begun an uprising against the German occupiers on 5 May; the Red Army arrived the day after the war in Europe ended, on 9 May. Following the German surrender, all of what had once been Czechoslovakia was occupied by the Red Army in line with agreements made by the Allied leaders in Yalta in February 1945.

This mural depicting the arrival of the Red Army in Prague is still in the station hall in Čierna nad Tisou in Slovakia, close to the border with Ukraine. Exactly when it was painted is unknown, but probably in the 1960s, as it features a spacecraft on the right.

Democracy replaced by communism

With the liberation of the country from German forces, and the removal of the Nazi puppet regime in Slovakia, Czechoslovakia was restored as an independent country in May 1945. However, it was a smaller country, as all of the eastern region of Ruthenia was incorporated into the Soviet Union and remains part of Ukraine today. The new government in Prague, led by Edvard Beneš, who had spent the war leading the exiled government in London, was determined that history would not repeat itself and issued decrees requiring the removal of all ethnic Germans, plus Hungarians, from Slovakia. These 'Beneš Decrees' led to a series of often violent and deadly expulsions in 1945–46, with large numbers of the German speakers expelled, moving to what would become West Germany, especially neighbouring Bavaria.

The Soviet leader Josef Stalin wanted a communist government in the new Czechoslovakia and the democratic government elected in 1946, led by Beneš, was overthrown in a coup by the Communist Party in February 1948. For the next 41 years, the Communist Party imposed one party rule, initially following a harsh political and economic policy based on Stalin's in the Soviet Union. A brief period of 'liberal' communist rule in 1968, with widespread freedoms for travel, media and political activity, followed Slovak Communist leader Alexander Dubček becoming the Czechoslovak Communist Party leader.

This period, known in the West as the 'Prague Spring', was overthrown in August 1968 by an invasion by Czechoslovakia's nominal allies in the Warsaw Pact, with Soviet troops and tanks forming the bulk of the half-million strong invasion force. Dubček resigned in 1969, and another

20 years of communist rule followed. In 1970s and 1980s, the government tried to offset a weakening economy by offering more consumer goods, while restricting political discussion and harassing political opponents.

Rail network rebuilt and modernised

National rail company ČSD was reconstituted from 9 May 1945, replacing the separate railway administrations run by the German occupiers and Slovak fascist government. ČSD embarked on a programme of modernisation, with the repair and reconstruction of war-damaged infrastructure in Slovakia and Moravia as a key priority. Most lines were repaired and reopened by 1947. Following the communist seizure of power, all remaining privately owned railways were nationalised and became part of ČSD on 1 January 1949.

Electrification using 3000V DC of the main line network was undertaken in the 1950s and early 1960s, with the Usti nad Labem–Prague–Olomouc–Bohumín–Žilina–Košice–Čierna nad Tisou route as the initial priority. In the Prague area, the 3000V DC system replaced the earlier 1500V DC electrification (in use since 1928) in 1962. Over the next three decades, most main routes were electrified with 25kV AC, which was preferred for new schemes from the mid-1960s onwards.

The result of the change from DC to AC led to some parts of the country needing dual voltage locos and multiple units where the two systems met and in the mid-1970s, the first dual voltage 3kV DC/25kV AC express locos, Class ES499.0 (now Class 350), were introduced. From the 1980s, larger numbers of lower-powered Class ES499.1 (now Class 363) dual voltage locos were also delivered by Škoda.

Between 1979 and 1990, over 400 locos sharing the same basic bodyshell were built by Škoda for ČSD. 3kV Class E499 (now Class 162/163) were delivered in green livery, while dual voltage Class ES499.1 were delivered in blue livery. Carrying both old and new numbers, E499 3046 (163 046-6) and 363 048-0 (ES499 1048) are seen at Praha střed depot on 14 April 1990.

Eastern Bloc loco builder

The Soviet-established Council for Mutual Economic Assistance (Comecon) allocated industrial and economic activities in the Soviet Bloc from 1949 with Czechoslovakia assigned a key role in the iron and steel industry. This had historically been based in Moravia, especially around Ostrava and Třinec, where existing plants were expanded. A major new steelworks was also built at Haniska, southwest of Košice in eastern Slovakia, and all this new heavy industry led to major growth in rail freight, with not just raw materials, but also finished steel, being transported.

The massive new Východoslovenské železiarne (East Slovakian Ironworks) plant near Košice opened in May 1966 and was supplied with iron ore directly from the Soviet Union via a new 87km 1,520mm gauge line built from Užhorod in Ukraine – the Širokorozchodná trať, meaning 'broad gauge track', abbreviated in Slovak to ŠRT. Initially diesel operated, this was electrified at 3000V DC in the early 1970s.

Comecon also assigned Czechoslovakia significant roles in supplying railway equipment to the entire Eastern Bloc; Škoda (whose main works in Plzeň was renamed after Soviet leader Lenin between 1953–65) supplied electric locomotives to multiple countries including the Soviet Union, while ČKD Lokomotivka (Českomoravská Kolben-Daněk), based in Prague, built over 12,800 diesel locos for export as well as supplying ČSD. The latter's ČKD Tatra subsidiary built over 24,000 trams for export as well as supplying Czechoslovak cities, and also provided large numbers of two-axle railcars for use by ČSD and by MAV in neighbouring Hungary.

A 1957 Závody Vladimíra Iljiče Lenin (Vladimir Ilyich Lenin Works) builder's plate on 1.5V DC loco E422 0000-3 (ČD 100 003) from the 1953–65 period, when the Plzeň Škoda Works carried Lenin's name.

Škoda exported thousands of electric locos to the Soviet Union and other Comecon member countries. Many were direct copies of locos built for ČSD, such as the 91 Class 42 locos (Škoda model 46E) sold to Bulgarian Railways (BDZ) in 1966–70, which were based very closely on the model 47E, built for ČSD at the same time (today's Classes 230/240). BDZ had withdrawn most of its Class 42 fleet by 2010; loco 42 077 is seen here at Ruse depot on 4 October 2011.

ČKD delivered 8,200 six-axle diesel locos to the ChME3 design between 1963 and 1994; the largest production run for a main line diesel design ever, most for export and almost all were built in Prague. ČSD had over 300 designated T669 (now Class 770/771). Two of the 7,459 delivered to the Soviet Union, ChME3 6494 and 6516, both delivered in 1989, are seen at Irkutsk, Russia, in June 1996. Despite the changes in Eastern Europe, the final 570 of these locos were delivered in 1990–91, with the last five built in 1994, ordered by newly independent Ukraine following the collapse of the Soviet Union, although the final two ended up in Estonia in 2002 after several years in store.

Velvet revolution

Following the fall of the Berlin Wall in November 1989, and the election of a democratic government in Poland earlier that year, the momentum for change grew across Eastern Europe. Major demonstrations were held in Prague and Bratislava. Václav Havel, a writer and opponent of the communist regime who had been jailed for political activity several times, led calls for a new government and after the communist regime gave way to demands for a democratic government without resorting to violence, Havel became the first president of the newly democratic Czechoslovakia in December 1989.

The country was established as a federal state, giving greater autonomy to Slovakia, in part recognising the differences in terms of history, language, and geography that the two halves of the country had. Former 'Prague Spring' Communist leader, Alexander Dubček, was elected chairman of the new federal Czechoslovak parliament at the end of 1989.

The end of communism, as seen at the ČSD loco depot in Kralupy nad Vltavou in early 1990, on a poster promoting a speech by former communist leader Gustáv Husák. Someone has written 'Komanistisley puč [communist putsch] 1948–1989 krach komanistu [communist collapse]'.

The new government faced an entirely new economic and political situation. To the north, the former East Germany was also in the process of not only replacing its communist government, but, by December 1989, there was already serious talk about Germany reunifying as a single country. Further east in Europe, in December 1989, there was deadly street fighting in Romanian cities while the Soviet Union was beginning to disintegrate, although it would be two years before it was formally defunct. The impact of the multiple changes in Eastern Europe was dramatic and particularly affected companies like Škoda and ČKD, which had relied on exports to the Comecon Bloc.

Pre-1989, all ČSD locos and multiple units had the red star on the front, but from December 1989 these were rapidly removed, as were communist symbols and propaganda at stations and depots. In this case, removing the red star badge has ironically revealed a painted one underneath! Seen here at Nymburk depot, 15 April 1990.

Velvet divorce

By 1992, it was clear that the new free Czechoslovakia was unlikely to survive, as the changes in Eastern Europe impacted the Czech part of the country differently from Slovakia. The Czech lands were nearer potential new export customers and job opportunities in West Germany or Austria. In contrast, Slovak heavy industry, most of which had been built as part of the Comecon planned economy, found it had lost customers abroad while the collapse of the USSR left Russia and the other former Soviet republics economically weakened but also determined to build their own indigenous industries to replace imports.

The result was GDP that was 20 per cent higher in the Czech regions by 1991, and the central government in Prague stopped subsidies that had been paid to Slovakia under the communist regime. Faced with demands for more centralised control from Prague, Slovak politicians began talks on independence as a looser confederation was judged to be impossible. Some in Slovakia promoted the attempt in 1919 to create a separate entity and the wartime 'independent' state as evidence that the country could go it alone. On 23 July 1992, Czech and Slovak politicians agreed that the country would be divided into two, and that this would happen on 1 January 1993.

The divorce process was entirely peaceful, with the media coining the description 'velvet divorce' as the successor to the 'velvet revolution' in 1989. The negotiators for both new countries agreed a pragmatic approach to dividing state-owned property, valuing it all at 475 billion Crowns and then dividing it based on population size. The new Czech Republic, with around 10 million people, was twice as large as Slovakia, so assets were split two to one. This also provided the basis for the division of state railway ČSD.

Since 1993, the two countries have remained partners and have generally good relations. Both joined the European Union in 2004, but while Slovakia adopted the Euro single currency in 2009, the Czech Republic has not, and most politicians have avoided setting any firm timescale to do so. Economically, both countries have diversified their economies and seen economic growth; many Slovaks now commute to work in neighbouring Austria, where wages are significantly higher. Public opinion surveys consistently show that people in both countries regret the break-up of Czechoslovakia.

Right: The Czech and Slovak Federative Republic was the country's name from April 1990 to the end of 1992, making it one of the shortest-lived peacetime countries in the world. This border sign is seen at the border with Germany in 1991.

Below: Most of the ČSD fleet was split up in 1992, based upon where it was used. As a result, all 50 Class E479/Class 131 double electric locos passed to Slovakia. Two years before the country split up, E479 1069 (131 069-7) and sister loco E479 1070 (131 070-5) pass Poprad Tatry on 4 April 1991.

Chapter 2

Railways in transition: 1989–93

When the new government replacing the Communist Party took power in Czechoslovakia on 10 December 1989, the national railway company ČSD gained new political masters. Initially little changed in practice, although railway employees who were no longer required to belong to Communist Party-approved trade unions started to organise independently. The most obvious initial manifestation of the change of regime was the removal of communist red stars from trains and propaganda from railway buildings. Organisational changes followed with ČSD being separated from the Ministry of Transport, and the Central Directorate of ČSD then established, which ran the railways until the country split in two in 1993.

ČKD-built 'goggles' locos 753 248 and 754 202 stand side by side at Děčín depot on 16 April 1990, one with its red star still in place and the other with fresh yellow paint where it used to be. 754 202 was one of two prototypes built in 1975 for the final 'goggles' type, the 1,472kW Class 754; 84 locos followed in 1979–80. 754 202 was renumbered as 750 409 and later in 2012, it was rebuilt with a new engine to become 750 711. 753 248 was one of 408 similar locos; it has also been rebuilt with a new engine and is now used by the Czech subsidiary of Polish freight operator PKP Cargo as 753 725.

New loco numbers

ČSD had begun renumbering its fleet in 1988, from a system developed immediately after World War One, where letters were used as a prefix to distinguish types of traction, for example E for electric and T for diesel, which by the 1980s had multiple prefixes, such as E for 3kV DC electric, S for 25kV AC or ES for dual voltage. The new system was like that used in both East and West Germany and employed six-digit computerised numbers that included a check digit to prevent incorrect data entry. This book will normally refer to the post-1988 class numbers, although as can be seen from the pictures, some locos retained the old numbers for several years or carried both as new cast metal plates with the new numbers were made to replace the old ones.

With both old and new numbers visible through the grime covering its maroon paint, T435 0040, aka 720 040-5, is seen at Kralupy nad Vltavou on 14 April 1990. ČKD built 150 of the T435 design for ČSD, which became Class 720 after 1988, while another 83 were sold to industrial users in Czechoslovakia, and others exported to East Germany (20 locos as DR Class 107), Albania, and Iraq. ČD withdrew its last Class 720 locos in 1995, but they remain in use with private operators, especially track maintenance companies.

By early 1990, Czechoslovakia's main trading partners in the Comecon Bloc were all, to varying degrees, undergoing rapid change, that for many people was not only unexpected but sometimes uncomfortable. Organisations that had spent decades specialising in exports of specific products within the Eastern Bloc found that suddenly their customers could not afford the products or had insufficient hard currency to pay for them, as countries revalued their currencies to adapt to the new situation. Czechoslovakia allowed its currency to float from April 1990, which for its businesses increased prices for some former Eastern Bloc customers, but overnight reduced them for Western customers. This threw a lifeline to some Czechoslovak companies, while increasing the cost of imports from the West, which in turn helped domestic competitors stay in business.

The 3kV DC 90km/h Class E469.2, later Class 122, was built by Škoda in 1967 and based on the earlier Class 121. Used almost exclusively for freight, class leader 122 001-1 is seen leaving Děčín with a chemical train on 16 April 1990.

Passenger services

In 1989, ČSD operated passenger services on almost every line in the country, with very few routes only used by freight trains. Exceptions included purpose-built industrial systems used mainly for coal mining in the north of Bohemia, around Most and in the Ostrava area. Passenger services were operated using a fairly modern fleet by contemporary Eastern European standards, with the majority of rolling stock built after 1960.

The most modern electric locos were the Class 163/363, most of which were ordered prior to the collapse of the communist regime, and which would continue to be delivered until 1992. New dual voltage 3kV DC/15kV AC Class 372 locos built for the planned electrification between Děčín and the East German border were delivered by Škoda from 1988, although the electrification was not inaugurated until June 1992. Twenty of this type were exported, being sold to Deutsche Reichsbahn as its Class 230, later becoming DB AG's Class 180.

Express passenger services were mainly in the hands of the 1978 vintage Class 150 and earlier 1973–74 Class 350 dual voltage locos, while the older Class 140/141 'Bobina' locos, built by Škoda in the 1950s, or more modern Class 130s were in use operating semi-fast and slower passenger services on the 3kV DC electrified network. Some passenger services were worked by the more modern 1970s-built centre cab Class 110/111 locos that were more normally found working empty stock or trip freights.

The most modern locos in the ČSD fleet were the large 3kV DC Class 162/163 and dual voltage (3kV DC/25kV AC) Class 363 electric fleets. These were nicknamed 'Pershing', after short range nuclear missiles deployed by NATO, as, when new, the locomotives had a high failure rate so were 'short range'! Despite this, they had good acceleration, again like missiles. One of the first '163s' dating from the mid-1980s, 163 019-3 is seen at Děčín hl.n on 16 April 1990 with a train for Prague. This loco has since been upgraded to 140km/h operation by swopping bogies and is now numbered 162 019-9.

After World War Two, ČSD's first electric locos were the Class 499.0 (later Class 140) Bo-Bo design built by Škoda, which used designs and technology licensed from Swiss manufacturers, SLM and Secheron; the original Swiss prototypes being the Bern-Lötschberg-Simplon Class Ae4/4, which were considered very advanced when introduced in 1944. The first ČSD loco, E499 001, was delivered in June 1953 and 99 more followed by 1958. An export version, designated ChS1, was sold to the Soviet Union and North Korea. By the 1980s, most Class 140s were in Slovakia, although some were based in Olomouc and survived long enough to enter ČD stock. On 4 April 1991, 140 051-4 in ČSD green livery is seen at Čadca, with a service to Bohumín.

The successor to the E499.0 design appeared in 1957. The Class E499.1 (later Class 141) design used a different body design, dispensing with the round windows (some of which opened) found on the earlier design. Between 1959 and 1961, 61 locos were delivered and most remained in service into the early 1990s, based entirely in what would become the Czech Republic. Škoda exported the design widely, 30 to neighbouring Poland (as PKP Class EU05) and 87 to the Soviet Union, classified ChS3, in 1960–61. 141 043-0 is seen at Ústí nad Labem hl.n on 1 April 1991, with the 11.50 service to Chomutov.

Express services on the more recently electrified lines, those using 25kV AC since the 1970s, were largely operated by dual voltage Class 363 and 350 locos with local services hauled by Class 230/240 or 242 AC only machines. Electric suburban services around major cities such as Prague, Brno, Bratislava, and Košice were partly operated by 3kV DC Class 451/452 EMUs dating from the mid-1960s, and later 1970s-built Class 460 3kV DC and Class 560 25kV AC units.

ČSD had two basic EMU types. The oldest were the Class 451/452 3kV DC four-car trains built between 1962–73 by Vagónka Studénka, which were ahead of their time and featured low floor areas, although this was more from necessity as most stations had no real platforms, as shown in this picture of 451 064-0 at Nymburk on 15 April 1990. The last Class 451 trains were withdrawn by ČD in 2018, two have been preserved.

Services on non-electrified lines were handled by both diesel locos and DMUs. Large numbers of Class 810 two-axle railcars plus trailer cars had been built by Vagónka Studénka at Studénka between 1973 and 1984. As these were much cheaper to operate than conventional loco-hauled trains, they had enabled large parts of the network to retain passenger trains; hundreds had also been exported to neighbouring Hungary. Smaller numbers of older and heavier Class 830/831 DMUs, built between 1949–60, were in use, as well as Class 850/851 trains, introduced in 1962–68.

In the early 1990s, there were hundreds of diesel locos used daily for passenger work, mostly Class 753/754 'goggles' locos, so called because their windscreens looked like swimming goggles. Totalling 488 examples and built between 1968–80, they worked all over the country. From 1991, the first Class 750 locos rebuilt with electric train heating, converted from Class 753s, appeared; this programme begun by ČSD survived the break-up of the country, with 165 being converted in 1991–95.

In 1963, ČSD had introduced a prototype six-axle 25kV AC Škoda-built loco numbered S699 001. Production of four-axle locos followed in 1966–70, these incorporating glass-fibre cabs which gave rise to the nickname 'Laminatka', while they were designated S489.0/S499.0 and later Classes 230 and 240. Class 230 passed to ČD in 1993, while Class 240 was split between both countries in 1993; the Czech machines have been used only for freight for a decade. In Slovakia, they still work passenger trains and 240 127-1, seen at Bratislava hl.st on 3 April 1991, was still in passenger service, working from Bratislava 30 years later in late 2020.

The later Class S499.02/Class 242 25kV AC locos used the bodyshell developed for exports to Bulgaria (BDZ Class 43/44) in the early 1970s, and a similar body was used for the 3kV DC ČSD Class 130 as well. Class S499.02/242 was the last 'classic' design delivered by Škoda and some of the last batches were built alongside the new standard Class 163/363 locos in 1981. After 1993, all Class 242 locos remained in the ČD fleet, although they routinely operated into Slovakia for many years. S499.0256 (242 256) is seen at Františkovy Lázně on 31 March 1991, with the 16.39 service to Prague.

The 20 Class ES499.0, later Class 350, dual voltage locos were introduced in 1973–75 to work fast trains on the Prague to Bratislava route, although it took 25 years from introduction before their top speed of 160km/h could actually be utilised, as initially the route was limited to 140km/h or less! One loco, ES499.0010, was written off when only a year old after a serious accident at Bratislava hl.st in June 1977. The last of the class, nicknamed 'Gorillas' by crews because of their 4000kW power rating, 350 020-4 is seen at Bratislava hl.st in the dual voltage blue livery used in the late 1980s–early 1990s, on 3 April 1991.

ČSD often assigned locos to particular crews, who then in turn 'customised' the loco cabs with curtains and decorations. 'Goggles' loco 753 394-6, seen at Děčín depot on 16 April 1990, has a bespoke handmade decoration on each end to replace the former communist red star, which features the Bohemian coat of arms with a silver lion dating from the 13th century.

Also commonly seen working passenger trains in the early 1990s were the 'Bartokda' Class 751/752, plus the first of the electric train heat equipped Class 749 conversions, 60 of which were converted in 1992–96. Class 749/751/752 are less powerful than the more modern 'goggles' locos using the 1,476hp (1103kW) ČKD K6S310 DR engine, which was also used in the ČSD Class 770/771 Co-Co design. This engine was also employed in the export ChME3 version, which was sold in huge numbers to the Soviet Union and other countries. The 'Bardotka' nickname had been coined by local railwaymen as the seven Class T478.0 prototype and pre-series batch dating from 1964–66 were curvaceous; Bardotka refers to Bridget Bardot, who was famous even in communist Czechoslovakia!

Smaller diesel loco types, such as Class 721, 730, 735 and 742, were also commonly used for secondary lines, sometimes with coaching stock and also in place of Class 810 railcars, hauling multiple trailers. Such work would remain common into the second decade of the 21st century, especially for Class 742 in the Czech Republic, but is now much rarer. The last main line diesel loco class delivered to ČSD was the 62-strong Class 731, delivered in 1988–92, although a follow-on order for 60 more was cancelled because of the break-up of Czechoslovakia.

Large numbers of trains on non-electrified routes were hauled by diesel locos with the various 'goggles' classes 753 and 754 being the most common. 753 387-0 is seen here arriving at Neratovice with the 16.20 Turnov–Praha–Vysočany service on 1 April 1991. On this loco, the former red star has been replaced by a ČSD badge and 'winged wheel' emblem. The smart, recently painted loco contrasts with the drab coaches behind it, which were typical at the time.

ČSD introduced new diesel-powered trains very quickly after World War Two. The first batch of 52 type M262.0, later Class 830, units were constructed by ČKD between 1949 and 1952 and eventually 238 were built by the time production ended in 1960. One of the first batch, M262 0027/830 027-9, was already 40 years old when photographed at Děčín depot on 16 April 1990.

The M286.0/Class 850 diesel units were the successors to the 1940s-designed M262/830. ČKD built 50 between 1962 and 1967, each equipped with a 515kW ČKD K12 V170 DR diesel engine; a second series of 37 units followed in 1966–67, with a more powerful 588 kW version of the engine, these later becoming Class 851. The units were used widely by ČSD and both ČD and ŽSR took them into their fleets. The units were designed to work with unpowered trailers, running round the train like a loco at terminus stations. 851 030-7, with two trailers, is seen at Poprad Tatry in Slovakia on 3 April 1991, with a service to Tatranska Lomnica.

The type M152.0, or Class 810, railcars were built in the 1970s in large numbers to enable final replacement of steam locos and to cut operating costs on many rural branch lines. Thanks to a simple design, they contributed to much of the passenger network remaining open at a time when Western countries, and even communist neighbours, were closing many lines. Vagónka Studénka built 678 between 1973 and 1982, each equipped with a 155kW LIAZ (Liberecké automobilové závody – 'Liberec Automobile Works') ML634 diesel engine used in contemporary buses. In addition, 912 un-powered 'Btax' trailers were built to the same basic design and used either between two power cars or hauled by a power car like a locomotive. Two units, 810 038 and 810 037, in the then current orange and yellow ČSD livery, are seen on 1 April 1991 at Neratovice.

Freight traffic plummets

The economy underwent major changes after 1989 and this directly impacted rail freight traffic. Privatisation of most major companies was undertaken, with car maker Škoda Auto sold to Volkswagen in 1991, which not only preserved jobs and factories in the short term, but, over the next three decades, provided a major source of rail freight traffic, supplying the car plants and exporting the finished cars. Most other major companies were privatised from 1992 onwards. The rest of the Škoda group, which largely specialised in rail engineering, was privatised in a complex series of often opaque transactions, but its previous major customers, such as Soviet Railways and even domestic ČSD, could not afford large new fleets of locomotives or trains, so the business contracted dramatically.

The other major rail engineering firm, ČKD (Českomoravská Kolben-Daněk), which included Tatra trams alongside highly successful diesel locomotive designs, fared even less well. Privatised in 1994, it was broken up in 1998, with many parts bankrupt, although Siemens acquired part of the company.

The outlook for the country's railways in the early 1990s was not good. Before 1989, Czechoslovakia had been dependent on heavy industry and equipment (including railway rolling stock) exports, mainly to the Comecon Bloc. Freight traffic went into rapid decline, falling by around 40 per cent between 1989 and 1992, with some traffic flows disappearing altogether. Investment in the rail network in the 1970s and 1980s, while superficially significant with new electrification and new locomotives, had avoided any major improvements to existing lines and as wages were low, relied on large numbers of employees rather than technology for activities such as track maintenance, level crossing operation and signalling.

ČSD served multiple industrial customers, even in small towns, so mixed trains of wagonload freight were commonplace. T466 0090, one of 299 type T466.0, later Class 735, diesel locos built in Slovakia by Turčianske strojárne Martin (TSM), is seen at Mladá Boleslav on 15 April 1990, with a freight that includes small containers in wagons designed for coal. TSM built many smaller diesel locos and some larger ones for ČSD, under license from ČKD. With the fall in freight traffic after 1990, many Class 735 locos were withdrawn as they were expensive to operate, although some were completely rebuilt as ČD Class 714 or ŽSR Class 736.

The sole P&O container on this train, passing north through Ústí nad Labem hl.n on 1 April 1991, was noteworthy as modern containers like this were rarely seen in Czechoslovakia before 1990. In 2021, multiple full length container trains pass through Ústí every day! The lack of specialist wagons means it is being carried on an ordinary bogie flat wagon. The loco hauling the train, 121 067-3, is one of 85 type E469.1s built by Škoda in 1960–61 for freight traffic. Most were withdrawn by 2010, although some remain in use with private freight operators.

Between 1961 and 1965, ČKD built 44 six-axle diesel electric locos; 17 designated T678.0 (later Class 775) and 27 as T679 (or Class 776) which were equipped with steam heating for passenger work. In the final maroon livery, T678 0002, one of the original prototypes from 1961, is seen at Poprad Tatry on 3 April 1991. Equipped with a 1,472kW ČKD 8 S 310 DR engine, the locos were powerful and judged to be successful; ČKD exported 20 of the T679.0 version to Iraq in 1964. However, Comecon policy, set in Moscow, determined that ČSD, like other Eastern Bloc railways, should buy the Soviet 'M62' design instead, and eventually 599 were purchased by ČSD and designated T679.1 (later Class 781). The Class 775/776 locos were all withdrawn by 1996, and three have survived in preservation.

ČSD had extensive fleets of shunting locos ranging from two-axle low powered diesels to four-axle trip and shunting locos. Three shunting locos are visible in this 15 April 1990 picture at Nymburk depot. On the left are two Class 702 shunters; 382 of which were built by TSM in Slovakia between 1967 and 1971. On the right is three-axle loco 710 048-0, one of 475 delivered by ČKD from 1961. These locos with hydrodynamic transmission were relatively rare by 1990, as withdrawals began in the mid-1980s. Both Class 702 and 710 types were extensively exported by ČKD and some remain in industrial use today.

Troubled future?

By the early 1990s, private car ownership was increasing rapidly as large numbers of cheap second-hand vehicles from neighbouring West Germany and Austria became accessible, which meant people could choose not to use trains. However, in 1991, ČSD introduced the first express trains branded using the, until then, Western European 'Eurocity' name on the Prague to Vienna route, as the first step towards improving long distance services.

For railway employees, there were multiple changes due to the collapse of the communist regime and, three years later, the division of the country, leading to a reduction in the number of people being employed. However, initially at least, there were few line closures or significant passenger service reductions, as successive governments either chose to subsidise operations or not demand cost savings that led to lines closing.

Compared to all neighbouring countries, this remains true in 2021, especially in the Czech Republic, although responsibility for local rail services is now largely devolved to regional government. Thirty years on, the prospects for rail freight have also changed beyond recognition, with multiple freight operators competing, and substantial transit traffic from the North Sea ports to south-eastern Europe, crossing both countries daily.

ČSD had a massive network of passenger lines, which were labour intensive and expensive to operate, with mechanical signalling and infrastructure that, in some cases, had barely changed in 80 years. In October 1995, DMUs 830 052 and 830 141, dating from the 1950s, by then operated by ČD, arrive at Rudná u Prahy with a service to Praha Smichov.

Chapter 3

Two countries – two railways: 1993–2003

Following the decision to split Czechoslovakia into the Czech Republic and Slovakia in July 1992, the national railway company ČSD was also divided between the two countries. While it was historically based in Prague, it had regional directorates, with the two in Slovakia, in Bratislava and Košice, forming the basis of the new Slovak national railway company Železnice Slovenskej republiky (ŽSR), which took over on 1 January 1993, based in Bratislava, the Slovak capital. In Prague, new Czech national operator, Českých drah (ČD), took over operations in its part of the former Czechoslovakia.

Fleet divided

The creation of two independent countries and two new national railways was relatively simple for the railway network itself, as it was either in one country or the other as the borders were not subject to any significant debate. However, the split led to rolling stock being divided between both countries, although there were exceptions, such as trains dedicated to certain lines for technical reasons, such as gauge or electrification type, or built for certain traffics, such as the entire Class 131 double electric locos, which remained in Slovakia. Generally, though, this was done on a two to one ratio with ČD receiving twice as much as ŽSR, although locomotives and multiple units largely remained at the depots they were already based at; the split reflected the denser and busier Czech network compared to the Slovak one.

The creation of two countries from one also meant the previous international railway number '54' for Czechoslovakia could no longer be used by both countries. Again, the pragmatic solution was taken, as ČD had more vehicles, the Czech Republic kept '54' while Slovakia was issued with the new country code, '56', by the UIC, meaning it had to renumber all of its coaches and wagons, a process that took over two years.

Splitting up ČSD in January 1993 led to rebranding in both countries, with ČSD removed and the new operators' logos added. The results were still visible several years later, as this picture taken in October 1995 shows. Longer term, both national rail operators developed their own new liveries to replace the ČSD ones.

ŽSR inherited less of the more modern electric locos, in part as many of them were 3kV DC Class 162/163, some only delivered in 1991, while much of the Slovak network, especially around Bratislava, was electrified at 25kV AC. While ŽSR retained all the 1980s vintage Class 131 double electric locos, it was also given ten of the 12 most modern Class 263 25kV AC locos; nearly 30 years later, ten are with ZSSK, while two are still used by ČD. ŽSR obtained part of the earlier 1968–70-built Class 240 fleet, while ČD retained all the older mid-1960s-built Class 230 locos.

The last ČD depot operating Class 140s was Olomouc, where the locos were used for short distance local services. 140 089-4, restored to a version of its original livery, is seen at Olomouc hl.n on 27 April 2004, with train Os14012, the 13.46 to Nezamyslice.

ŽSR retained a larger fleet of the original Škoda-built 'Bobina' Class 140 locos, dating from the mid-1950s, than ČD, which had some based at Olomouc. Some of the Slovak locos survived into the 21st century and are still in use with freight operators in 2021! The diesel fleet was divided largely based on where locos had been historically based. ŽSR inherited the small fleets of powerful ČKD-built Class 775 and 776 six-axle diesel locos, while the far more numerous Soviet-built Class 781 fleet was divided between ŽSR and ČD.

The large fleets of diesel multiple units and smaller EMU classes were divided based upon where they were used in 1992. As a result, most DMU classes were shared between the two countries, while ČD retained all the 3kV Class 451/452 EMUs, mainly used around Prague. Coaches, wagons, and civil engineering trains were also divided largely based upon where they were based or for internationally used stock on the overall two to one basis.

Despite the division of the rail network into two new companies, large numbers of mainly diesel locos remained in industrial use. This included the very large Class 740 fleet built by ČKD between 1973 and 1989; 459 were built for Czechoslovak industrial users and another 161 exported to Poland for use by industry there.

Two 1970 Škoda classic designs meet at Kynšperk nad Ohří on 11 May 2009. 242 208-7 arrives with train Os7012, the 12.17 Klášterec nad Ohří–Cheb, while in the foreground is a Škoda 110 car. The car was mass produced in Mladá Boleslav in the mid-1970s when the Class 242 fleet were also being built in Plzeň. All the Class 242s remained with ČD after 1993 but have now been partially withdrawn. The Škoda Auto business remains one of the key parts of the Czech economy, exporting thousands of vehicles, mostly by rail, in the 21st century.

Crews for loco 781 095-5 change over at Mladá Boleslav on 15 April 1990. The loco was one of the large fleet of 599 Soviet-built 'M62' diesel electric locos designated T679.1 (later Class 781) delivered to ČSD between 1966 and 1979 by Voroshilovgrad Locomotive Works in Luhansk, Ukraine. The M62 design, used primarily for freight, was expensive to use and consumed substantially more fuel than comparable locos, so ČSD and its successors, like DR/DB in East Germany, rapidly withdrew the type when freight traffic declined after 1990. Almost all Class 781 locos were withdrawn by 2000, although some were sold for further use in neighbouring countries, and a small number have been preserved.

ŽSR – Slovakia

In Slovakia, ŽSR was created almost from scratch from the Slovak part of ČSD. What had been regional divisions of the Czechoslovak company found themselves operating as the national railway company with very little time to prepare. Perhaps not surprisingly, the initial transition was difficult. Nine months after it was created, the new Slovak government legally defined ŽSR's role as a state-owned company and set out longer term reforms, such as the separation of infrastructure costs from train operations and allowed access to the network for operators from other countries; the most prevalent of which, initially, was ČD in the Czech Republic.

Slovakia, like all the other central European former Communist Bloc countries, had decided early on that it wanted to join the European Union, and during the 1990s took multiple steps to prepare for that happening. By 1996, the government had signed up to incorporating Slovakia in the developing trans-European freight and passenger rail corridors being promoted by the EU. Over the next three decades, this decision would result in substantial EU-funded investment in parts of the Slovak rail network.

In 1993, the 3,661km long Slovak rail network was in poor overall condition. Even on main lines, the top speed possible was very low, with 100km/h only achievable on under 20 per cent of the entire system as, under the communist regime, transport of heavy freight had been prioritised over passenger journey times. The only track in the country suitable for 140km/h operation was two sections of the 155km, 25kV AC electrified Kúty–Bratislava–Nové Zámky line.

In 1993, the majority of the electrified network in Slovakia used 3kV DC with the newly international Bohumín (Czech Republic)–Žilina–Košice route as the main artery. Alongside older electric locos, ŽSR had a fleet of more modern Class 162/163 locos, as well as some of their dual voltage Class 363 sisters. Fifteen years after independence, ZSSK loco 162 006-1 still carries the former ČSD 'DC' livery of green and yellow, being recorded at Žilina on 7 November 2018.

In 1996, the first steps towards sectorisation of ŽSR were taken with separate passenger, freight and rolling stock maintenance businesses being established. By the late 1990s, a policy of refurbishing and rebuilding some rolling stock was beginning to show results, with modernised intercity coaches appearing, while the first Class 811 DMUs rebuilt from the ČSD Class 810 design appeared in 1995; some of these used new bodyshells, others were converted from both powered and trailer Class 810 vehicles. From 2001, even more rebuilt units appeared, this time classified as Class 812 and all 64 were delivered by 2008.

In January 2002, ŽSR was split into two, with ŽSR remaining as the national rail infrastructure manager and new train operating company Železničná spoločnosť (ZSSK) taking over passenger and freight operations. Owing to low passenger revenue and a lack of sufficient government financial support, ZSSK removed passenger services on 24 regional and branch lines in February 2003, although some reopened shortly afterwards with regional government funding. Some of the others followed later or now have summer weekend trains, but most of the lines concerned have not reopened to passengers.

In 2003, just before Slovakia joined the EU, a small batch of six Stadler-designed GTW2/6 DEMUs were delivered as Class 840, these being assembled in Slovakia from parts supplied from Stadler's Swiss factories. No more were ordered, though, as rebuilding older units was considered more cost effective than buying new ones for the next decade.

For freight traffic, some older diesel designs were rebuilt, with the first Class 736 rebuilds of Class 735 locos appearing in 1998, and by 2008, 33 locos had been converted. Between 1998 and 2002, ten Class 771 locos were rebuilt with new engines and low bonnets to Class 773. No more followed and in 2009, the entire class was re-gauged to work in terminals on the 1,520mm gauge line, connecting the steelworks near Košice with Ukraine.

ŽSR inherited two batches of EMUs from ČSD; the 3kV DC Class 460 used around Košice and around a third of the 17 25kV AC Class 560 version used around Bratislava. Four of the Košice Class 460 fleet are seen there on 9 September 2005, carrying the new white and cream livery introduced by ŽSR.

Recently rebuilt ZSSK 812 038-8, converted from 810 437, and modernised trailer car 011 627-7, also in the same new Class 812 livery, were photographed at Poprad Tatry on 3 July 2010.

A third of the Stadler-built Class 840 fleet in one picture! ZSSK 840 004-6 and 840 005-3 are seen at Levoča on 3 July 2010. The short branch line to Levoča lost its regular passenger services from Spišská Nová Ves from 2 February 2003, as part of newly created ZSSK's service cuts. Due to the Basilica just outside Levoča being the site of a major annual pilgrimage on the Catholic Feast of the Visitation (normally on 2 or 3 July each year), the railway line now only has services during the pilgrimage days!

Between 1998 and 2008, 29 Class 735 locos were converted to Class 736 at Zvolen with new 1080kW Caterpillar 3512 DI-TA engines; 24 as Class 736.0 for freight and five as Class 736.1 for passenger services. The picture shows 736 020-9 and another 736.0 at Vrútky on 2 February 2015 with a freight.

Already a historic picture, newly converted 773 007-0 (formerly 771 125) at Zvolen depot on 10 September 2005. Ten Class 773.0 were converted from Class 771 in 1998–2002 and based at Zvolen. In 2009–10, all ten were converted to 1,520mm gauge as Class 773.8 with Russian-style SA3 buckeye couplers; 773 007-0 became 773 803-2.

ČD – Czech Republic

The Czech Republic followed a similar basic approach to that taken in Slovakia. New national railway operator, Českých drah (Czech Railways or ČD), took over from January 1993. By picking a name that used some of the old ČSD acronym, the cost of replacing 80,000 cast metal ownership plates on ČD's new fleet was avoided. Instead, maintenance staff used grinders to remove the 'S'. Such plates can still be seen in use on coaches and wagons 30 years later!

The Czech rail network, at 9,454km, was nearly three times bigger than the Slovak one and accounted for much more of the former ČSD's traffic. Just like Slovakia, line speeds were low with 120km/h the maximum, except for the Brno–Břeclav line, where speeds of up to 140km/h had been permitted since 1988. Decisions taken in the early 1990s led to substantial investment in improving main lines with work beginning from 1993 to rebuild for 160km/h and, in some places, completely realign the lines from Kolín to Česká Třebová, and then on to Olomouc and Brno.

Ambitious plans to undertake such work on all main lines never materialised. As an example, work to rebuild (again with multiple new faster sections of line) the Prague to České Budějovice and Linz line is expected to be completed in the early 2020s, while planning is still underway for the Choceň to Ústí nad Orlicí section of the Česká Třebová–Olomouc line, with an entirely new route with two major tunnels planned for construction in the mid-2020s.

Like Slovakia, the Czech Republic quickly decided to pursue EU membership, and began the process of restructuring its railway industry to meet EU rules and maximise future opportunities. In 2003, a new national operating company was formed, also known as ČD, but with the subtle name change to České dráhy. The rail network was transferred, along with the new infrastructure manager, Správa železniční dopravní cesty (Railway infrastructure administration or SŽDC), in 2003, but most employees remained with ČD; the more practical split transferring thousands of operating staff to SŽDC did not happen until 2011. Responsibility for funding rail services in the Czech Republic has moved to the country's regional governments in the last decade, and in a relatively small number of cases, this has led to lines losing passenger services, although some other lines closed before 1990 have reopened.

The last locos to be built at ČKD's historic factory were the 13 ČD Class 708s. When new, these worked some passenger trains, although all are now relegated to shunting work. In this picture, 708 004-7 had just arrived at Strakonice, on the Plzeň–České Budějovice main line, on 1 October 2007, with train Os18125, the 14.54 ex Vimperk.

ČD, like its neighbour ŽSR, inherited a fleet of locos and multiple units that was designed to support the heavy industrial economy of the Communist Bloc. Funds for investment in new rolling stock were very limited, and for several years, almost no new locomotives or multiple units were bought. ČD did buy 13 two-axle Class 708 diesel locos from ČKD from 1995 onwards, which were used to replace older Class 735 locos working both passenger and freight. The last of these, 708 013, was the final loco built by ČKD at its historic 'Lokomotivka' Praha Libeň factory. Other Class 735 locos were rebuilt to the new Class 714 design between 1993 and 1997, again for light passenger and freight use.

In order to maximise use of new 160km/h stretches of rebuilt line, 14 Class 150 locos were rebuilt between 1996 and 2002 for 160km/h operation. Larger numbers of 120km/h Class 163 and 363 locos were also rebuilt to 140km/h Class 162/362 versions.

In the early 1990s, ČD decided it wanted to buy tilting trains for services between Prague and Vienna or Berlin and ordered ten trains from a consortium led by ČKD. The plan came to nothing as ČKD became bankrupt. Eventually, seven 'Pendolino' trains, based on the Italian ETR470 model, were ordered from Fiat Ferroviaria, which itself was bought by Alstom in 2000, before the seven-car trains were delivered. After lengthy delays, the tri-voltage (3kV DC/15 and 25kV AC) Class 680 trains entered service in 2005 on ČD's most important domestic route between Prague and Ostrava, these operating a new all-reservation service branded as 'SuperCity'. Plans to use them in Germany came to nothing, although they did operate to Vienna for some years. To enable trains from the Czech Republic to reach Summerau in Austria, three Class 240 25kV AC locos were converted to dual 15kV/25kV AC in 2001–04.

One of the three Class 340 locos converted for use under 15kV AC catenary, although power under this voltage is limited to 1,200kW. 340 062-9 is seen at České Budějovice on 3 February 2007, with the 12.09 service to Linz, which it will work as far as Summerau, just across the border.

ČD inherited all 26 remaining Class 150 locos in 1993 (one was written off in 1981, when only three years old). 150 016-4, seen at its home depot of Praha Střed/Masarykovo on 25 October 1995, was one of 14 of the class rebuilt by Škoda to 160km/h as Class 151 in 1996–2002, being renumbered as 151 016-3. On the right is Class 141 pioneer and celebrity loco, 141 001-8.

One of the rebuilt Class 151 locos, 151 020-5 is seen speeding through Choceň on 30 September 2007, with international express 'Eurocity' train EC108, the 07.11 from Kraków, Poland, to Prague. The Class 151 will have replaced a Polish loco at Bohumín.

In service for around a year when this picture was taken on 21 April 2006, new 'Pendolino' led by 681 003-0 rounds the curve at Hranice na Moravě, working 'SuperCity' service SC501, the 05.56 Praha hl.n to Ostrava. A decade later, this unit was involved in a deadly level crossing collision at Studénka on 22 July 2015, when it hit a truck loaded with metal that had stopped on the crossing, killing three people, and severely damaging the train.

A variety of the diesel locos inherited by ČD can be seen in this 25 October 1995 view at Praha Vršovice depot. From left to right, 742 383-3 and 749 218-4 were both types used in large numbers nationwide in the 1990s. The modern looking 799 003-9 is a diesel/battery loco that was built at Jihlava in 1994, on the frames of older loco 700 116, which originally looked like 700 101-9 on the right. In total, 41 Class 799s were built using Class 700/701/702 locos as donors. ŽSR, like ČD, could not afford new shunting locos in the 1990s and also converted Class 701/702 locos to a very similar battery/diesel design, but classified them as 'electric' Class 199.

For suburban services, ČSD had bought two prototype double-decker EMUs; the two Class 470 trains, which entered service in 1991–92, had single-deck driving coaches and double-deck trailers – a configuration that was unusual in the 1990s, but is now widespread! Both units were withdrawn by 2009. Based on the experience gained with the Class 470, a new all double-deck design was developed. Known as ČD Class 471, and branded as 'CityElefant', the first sets entered service in 1997 and subsequent orders have taken the fleet to 83 trains, which have replaced large numbers of 1960s and 1970s ex-ČSD EMUs, as well as loco-hauled trains. The design, which features aluminium car bodies, has been an export success for manufacturer Škoda, which has old them in Slovakia, Lithuania, and Ukraine, plus loco-hauled coaches based on the same design in Slovakia and Germany.

Škoda delivered the Class 471 'CityElefant' double-deck EMUs in multiple batches, with deliveries staggered, as ČD could not then afford to buy multiple trains at once. When photographed at Praha Masarykovo station on 9 April 2004, 471 012-5 was only a few weeks old, and was about to leave with train Os9323, the 11.30 to Kolín.

Chapter 4
EU membership and fleet development

After the Czech Republic and Slovakia joined the EU on 1 January 2004, both national railway operators started to access substantial regional development funds that could be used to modernise existing trains and, in some cases, buy new ones. Over the next decade and a half, ČD and ZSSK, which, in 2004, still operated a fleet made up of essentially the same train types, developed their fleets in different ways, although some of the new designs are also common to both countries.

ČD bought 20 new 200km/h Class 380 multi-system locos from Škoda in 2004, originally for use into Germany, but this did not happen. Despite being due in service by 2007, the first loco entered traffic in 2010, and while the class has operated into Austria and Hungary, it was not used for services to Germany. ZSSK bought two similar, but 160km/h-rated, Class 381 locos. ČD put the entire Class 380 up for sale in late 2020, announcing plans to buy 90 modern electric locos and lease up to 50 more, these being in addition to the ten Siemens 'Vectron' MS locos it has leased from European Locomotive Leasing since late 2017.

The expansion of international freight and passenger services since 2004, with multiple private or foreign train operators, has led to several European standard loco designs, such as the Bombardier 'Traxx', the Siemens 'Eurosprinter' (German Class 189), 'Eurorunner' diesel and, more recently, Siemens' 'Vectron' electric design becoming common in both countries.

Electric traction developments

Extensive modernisation projects have been carried out by both ČD and ZSSK to extend the life and reliability of ex-ČSD fleets. The Class 163/363 electric loco fleets have been subject to significant change, with ČD Cargo rebuilding 30 Class 163 3kV DC locos to dual voltage Class 363.5 (3kV DC/25 kV AC) between 2010 and 2013. Most ČD passenger Class 363 120km/h dual voltage locos have been upgraded to 140km/h Class 362 standards by swapping bogies with faster Class 162 locos, which in turn have been reclassified Class 163 and, in many cases, sold to freight subsidiary ČD Cargo, as new EMUs had replaced their passenger work.

ČD dual voltage (3kV DC/15kV AC) loco 371 002, designed for services to Germany, crosses the Negrelli Viaduct over the River Vltava in central Prague on 12 April 2004, with a service from Děčín. This is currently the longest railway bridge in the Czech Republic and dates from 1849; the viaduct was completely rebuilt between 2017 and 2021. Class 371, a re-geared 160km/h version of the original Class 372, was the main traction for international services between Prague and Dresden from the late 1990s until 2017, when new leased Siemens 'Vectron' MS locos replaced them. Since 2018, Class 371s have been redeployed, operating domestic express services.

The first 25kV AC electric fleet, the ČSD 'Laminatka' S489, later Class 230, all passed to ČD in 1993 and initially were used for both passenger and freight trains. From December 2007, with the creation of ČD Cargo as a separate business within ČD, all the Class 230 locos were assigned to the freight business, with all the later Class 242 25kV AC locos allocated to the new passenger-only ČD. A few months before the class lost its passenger work, 230 100-0 was photographed at Havlíčkův Brod on 14 August 2007, with train Os14841, the 12.15 to Jihlava.

One consequence of the modernisation of the loco fleet dating from the 1980s–90s has been the withdrawal of many older 3kV DC locos built in the 1960s, although some have been sold for further use by private operators. The Czech government decided in December 2016 that all 3kV DC electrified routes should be converted to 25kV AC in a programme to be implemented between 2025 and 2040. As a result, 3kV DC electric locos will become increasingly redundant in the 2030s, unless more are rebuilt to dual voltage. In 2020, ČD Cargo introduced the first of ten Class 388 'Traxx' MS3 quadri-voltage (1.5kV/3kV DC and 15kV/25kV AC) locos on order from Bombardier, with an option for up to 40 more. The locos will be used in all neighbouring countries and Hungary.

ČD Cargo rebuilt 30 Class 163 3kV DC locos to dual voltage Class 363.5 (3kV DC/25 kV AC) between 2010 and 2013. These were delivered in the operator's new two-tone blue livery. 363 502-6, seen heading north through Zábřeh na Moravě on 10 February 2018, was built as one of the first prototype batch of the new type E449.3 (Class 163) locos, becoming 163 004 in 1988. In 2020, ČD Cargo announced plans to convert another 18 Class 163 locos to dual voltage; they and the existing ČD Cargo Class 163/363 fleet will also be equipped with European Train Control System (ETCS), which will become mandatory across the Czech Republic from 2025.

EU membership and fleet development

In Slovakia, ZSSK has followed a similar path by rebuilding Class 163 locos into new dual voltage machines, classified Class 361. The initial batch of five Class 361.0 locos were 140km/h, but the later batch of 21, designated Class 361.1, are capable of 160km/h and widely used on services where this speed can be achieved, such as between Žilina and both Bratislava and Prague (see front cover picture). Slovakia is also planning to phase out 3kV DC electrification and has already converted some parts of the Bratislava–Žilina route to 25kV AC. Like ČD, ZSSK has also leased new Siemens 'Vectron' MS locos, numbered as Class 383.1, since 2019.

Right: ZSSK leased ten Siemens 'Vectron' MS locos, designated Class 383, from Slovak firm, S Rail Lease, in 2018, and now uses them for all principal domestic trains, with some working to and from Vienna as well. In the overall red livery applied to all the locos, 383 109-6 arrives at Leopoldov on 8 November 2018, with train R600, the 04.07 Košice–Bratislava.

Below: ZSSK ordered two of the new Škoda type F109E (ČD Class 380) in 2009 and they were delivered in 2012. The Slovak locos are used for regional trains around Bratislava, where they are based. 381 001-7 is seen arriving at Bratislava hl.st on 6 July 2014, with a train of Škoda-built double-deck coaches, which are based on those used in the 'CityElefant' EMU design (ZSSK Class 671).

ČD 380 004-2, in Škoda Auto advertising livery, arrives at Bratislava hl.st on 6 July 2018, with 'Eurocity' train EC 276, the 11.41 Budapest Nyugati–Praha hl.n,, which it has worked from the Hungarian capital. The loco is advertising the new Škoda Karoq car and has the green Škoda logos used by Škoda Auto. The now completely separate railway engineering firm, Škoda Transportation, uses the same logo, but in blue.

Brand new dual voltage 'RegioPanter' 651 016-8 at Nepomuk on 31 March 2019, one of a batch bought for regional services around Plzeň that have a special regional livery to reflect this. In Slovakia, ZSSK has also ordered the RegioPanter design with 25 Class 660 trains to be delivered (13 three-car and 12 four-car) for use operating services around Žilina and Trenčín. Škoda built the first two trains delivered in 2019, with the rest being assembled in Slovakia at ŽOS Trnava. The last of the 25 trains are due to be delivered in 2022.

Diesel fleets modernised and reduced

ČD also rebuilt some of its diesel fleet with two Class 753 'goggles' locos dramatically converted to Class 755 with new loco bodies in 2005, but no more were ordered. From 2008, 30 Class 753 locos were rebuilt as Class 753.7 by CZ Loko, with new 1500kW Caterpillar 3512B engines; the conversion was funded by Dutch bank, ING Lease, who then leased the locos back to ČD Cargo.

From 2010, 19 more locos were modernised, this time ČD-owned Class 750, which were rebuilt to Class 750.7, with the 1550kW Caterpillar 3512C engine; again, this work was funded by a leasing company, this time from Austria, with the locos leased back to ČD.

Rebuilding ČKD-designed locos has been a core business for CZ Loko in Česká Třebová for many years, and multiple rebuilt locos are in use with Czech private operators. In the last decade, CZ Loko has also sold increasing numbers of new diesel locos to both ČD (Class 794 shunters) and ČD Cargo (Class 744), as well as exporting new and rebuilt locos all over Europe.

In Slovakia, very similar rebuild programmes for the 'goggles' loco types produced ten Class 756 conversions from Class 750/753 for ZSSK Cargo; these were rebuilt between 2008 and 2010 using the same 1500kW Caterpillar 3512B engine used in the Czech Class 753.7. From 2010, 25 passenger Class 757 locos were rebuilt from Class 750, with the Caterpillar 3512C engine used in the ČD Class 750.7 conversions. ZSSK Cargo also has 17 Class 746 locos, these being rebuilt from Class 742 with new bodywork and a 970kW Caterpillar 3508B engine.

New diesel-powered passenger trains have been ordered in both countries, some as recently as 2021. These include ČD Class 844 'RegioShark', built by Pesa in Poland, plus Stadler-built Class 840/841 'RegioSpider' railcars, and ZSSK Class 861 built by ŽOS Vrútky. In addition, second-hand modern DMUs from German operators are now widely used, especially in the Czech Republic; ČD and private operators have both leased and bought Stadler 'Regioshuttle' DMUs from German operators since 2015. Other imported trains, which are typically no more than 20 years old, have been used to replace older ex-ČSD designs; for example, ČD bought 12 ex-DB Class 646 Stadler GTW2/6 DMUs in 2020 for use around Olomouc.

Non-rebuilt Class 753 locos are now largely extinct, with a handful in private use or preserved. Two of the last examples in use with ČD Cargo, 753 229-4 and 753 187-4, are seen on a very cold evening in Liberec on 14 December 2010 with a freight.

The popular Czech Class 749 diesel locos, converted from Class 751/752 in 1992–96 by fitting them with electric train heating equipment, were due to be withdrawn at the end of 2013, but this did not happen in the end. Small numbers remain with ČD, but others are now with private operators and some of them work regular summer weekend trains from Prague, even in 2021. One of the ČD locos, 749 121-0, brings an empty stock train of East German-built double-deck coaches into Praha hl.n on 2 March 2013, with another Class 749 on the rear.

ČD still uses the more modern 'goggles' Class 754, plus the rebuilt Class 750.7 fleet, for passenger services on many non-electrified routes. In a unique orange and grey livery, 754 050-3 is seen leaving Hradec Králové hl.n after taking over from an electric loco on 3 May 2018, with train R923 from Prague to Trutnov. On the right is the first of the Class 750.7 rebuilt fleet, 750 701-5, which was converted from 750 368 in 2010.

New ČD Cargo 744 112-4 at Břeclav on 17 December 2019. ČD Cargo ordered five brand new 'Effishunter 1000' Class 744 diesel locos with 895kW Caterpillar C32 engines and Siemens traction equipment from Česká Třebová-based CZ Loko. The same manufacturer is also rebuilding older diesels for ČD Cargo, with up to 50 Class 742 locos to be rebuilt to a similar standard as the new Class 744-designated 'Effishunter 1000M' ('M' meaning modernised), these being renumbered as Class 742.71 from 742 711 upwards.

The 17 ZSSK Cargo Class 746 locos were rebuilt by CZ Loko using mostly ex-ČD Class 742 locos as donors for frames and bogies. Rebuilt with a new 970kW Caterpillar 3508B engine, the locos are mostly used from Zvolen and further east. ZSSK Cargo 746 003-3 (rebuilt from 742 060) is seen at Lučenec on 16 May 2011.

ZSSK has 25 Class 757 locos, rebuilt from Class 750 between 2010 and 2015 at ZOS Zvolen. The class leader, 757 001-3, is seen at Košice on 4 July 2018, with a service for Zvolen. The Class 757 rebuild programme was comprehensive and means the locos are readily identifiable as all the round bodyside windows were replaced by new flat body panels.

ČD modernised large numbers of the former Class 810 railcars and Class 010 trailers. Between 2005 and 2012, 110 two-car and 26 three-car Class 814 trains, branded 'Regionova', were created by rebuilding the older vehicles, adding through gangways and completely new interiors. 814 094-9 is seen at Olomouc-Řepčín on 5 December 2012, in the new yellow livery all units carried when delivered; some now have the new ČD blue and white or regional liveries.

ČD ordered a second batch of two-car DMUs from Polish manufacturer Pesa in March 2021, with 33 trains due in service from 2023 and options for up to 127 more. This order followed the first batch of 31 delivered in 2012–14. One of these, 844 024-0, arrives at Skalna on 2 July 2014, with a service from Luby u Cheby to Cheb.

In Slovakia, ZSSK has bought new Class 861 articulated diesel units, branded 'Regiomover', from domestic manufacturer ŽOS Vrútky, with 39 three-car and 14 two-car trains delivered between 2010 and 2021, these replacing older DMUs and loco-hauled trains. 861 013-5 is seen in Košice on 4 July 2018, with a service for Humenné.

Chapter 5

Central European rail freight hub

Since 1989, rail freight in the former Czechoslovakia has undergone major changes. The newly independent Czechoslovakia had legal rights to part of Hamburg Docks, thanks to the Treaty of Versailles, but, following World War Two, ČSD had re-routed traffic away from Hamburg by the late 1940s, as it was no longer readily accessible, due to the division of Germany. The same applied to the traditional 'Austro-Hungarian' Adriatic port of Trieste, which from 1945, was in Italy. Instead, ports in Yugoslavia became the preferred destinations.

The lack of regular international traffic between the Eastern Bloc and ports on the North Sea coast resulted in Czechoslovak exports to non-Comecon countries heading south through Hungary, rather than Austria. After 1989, the country began to reorientate itself towards its Western neighbours and this trend accelerated in the 1990s, after the division of Czechoslovakia into two countries.

Road freight also took advantage of the fall of former Iron Curtain borders and the volume of traffic on the roads north of Prague entering Germany caused the Germans to insist it was transferred to rail. A 'Rollende Landstrasse' ('Rolling Road' or RoLa) service carrying trucks was introduced by ČD in September 1994, from Lovosice, north of Prague, to Dresden, thereby removing trucks from the Labem/Elbe valley routes. The RoLa service, which ran 12 times daily each way, was only viable as the German state of Saxony subsidised it, and it ceased operation shortly after the Czech Republic joined the EU, as trucks could no longer be forced to use it under EU rules.

Since the late 1990s, both countries have allowed the creation of private rail freight companies, these competing with the national operators. As a result, ZSSK Cargo and ČD Cargo were established as independent companies with dedicated locomotive fleets in 2005 and 2007, respectively. The proliferation of new entrants has led to a vibrant market, with multiple operators on some routes using a wide variety of often second-hand locomotives.

Large industrial companies often had substantial railway operations, both within their own sites but also permitted on the ČSD system for short distances. Some of these operators, for example OKD (the subsidiary of mining company Ostravsko-karvinské doly) or TSS (formerly a ČD-owned track maintenance company), have developed into major rail freight companies offering their services more widely, and some have subsequently been bought by international investors.

ČD Cargo veteran loco 122 021-9, in the operator's current corporate blue livery, heads north with a train of brand new Škoda cars bound for Germany at Všetaty on 26 June 2016; the 3kV DC loco will work the train as far as Děčín, where a multi-voltage loco will replace it. With plans to convert the DC electrified network to 25kV AC, and the requirement to use ETCS, older 3kV DC locos like this will soon become a much rarer sight.

Industrial operators, such as the large Ostrava-based OKD, have become major rail freight operators. In 2008, OKD was still primarily focussed on coal transport. One of its extensive fleet of ČKD-built diesels, 740 673-9 is seen in Ostrava, at the city's main power station coal unloading terminal on 13 August 2008.

OKD acquired Viamont Cargo in 2008 and was renamed Advanced World Transport (AWT). Some of the Class 740 fleet were rebuilt by CZ Loko as Class 741, with new Caterpillar engines and rebuilt cabs. Two of these locos, 741 501-4 and 741 504-5, are seen on 11 April 2018 at Kolín, with empty car wagons. The leading loco has the original Viamont livery, while the second one is in AWT's orange scheme. In 2015, AWT was taken over by Polish freight operator PKP Cargo.

TSS (Traťová strojní společnost – Track Machine Company) was the former track maintenance division of ČD. It was privatised in 2011, and sold to Czech investors, who in 2016, announced they were selling 80 per cent of TSS Cargo to two Chinese companies. TSS has augmented the large diesel fleet it already had by buying all the remaining German (DB) Class 180 3kV DC/15kV AC electric locos when DB put these up for sale. The locos were built by Škoda at the same time as ČSD Class 372. At least one of the ex-DB locos now has TSS livery, with 180 020-0 seen stabled at Děčín on 8 July 2017.

This Bulgarian-registered electric loco appears to be ex-BDŽ 45 148; it is in fact ex-ČD 242 218, which has been re-registered using a spare number in the BDŽ series (as the original 45 158 is not in use). When seen passing through Bratislava hl.st on 6 July 2018, it was leased to Austrian open access operator LTE by the privatised Slovak railway works, ŽOS Zvolen. Bizarrely, there are also a handful of locos numbered as 'Czech' Class 242, which are in fact very similar ex-BDŽ Škoda-built Class 43 locos, dating from the early 1970s, which have been re-registered as Class 242!

Transit traffic booms

Since joining the EU, both countries now form a key part of the core Trans-European Transport Network (TEN-T), in particular these corridors which connect major ports and cities:

- Orient–East Mediterranean links the north German ports with Greek and Bulgarian ports via the Czech Republic and Slovakia, primarily using the Dresden–Prague–Břeclav–Bratislava corridor.
- Baltic–Adriatic links the ports of northern Poland with Adriatic ports in Italy, including Venice, mainly via Ostrava and Žilina–Vienna.
- Rhine–Danube links central Germany and eastern France with both Ukraine and the Black Sea ports in Romania and Bulgaria via Plzeň, Prague and Žilina, although other parallel corridors run entirely within Austria.

Under EU funding plans, these routes are to be equipped with modern ETCS cab signalling, enabling trains using modern multi-system locomotives to operate without stopping at national borders, thereby reducing transit times, and improving competitiveness with road or water transport. The development and use of the TEN-T routes has driven an increase in rail freight transiting both the Czech Republic and Slovakia. Before the pandemic, Slovakia recorded a 35 per cent increase in the volume of transit freight traffic between 2017 and 2019 alone, reaching 15.2 million tonnes and representing 3.8 billion tonne/kms, itself an increase of 22 per cent from 2017.

In the last decade, the EU-wide licensing of locomotives has become simpler, although it remains much more complex than the system for lorries! This has allowed more and varied locos from neighbouring countries to become a common sight, these often routinely seen hundreds of kilometres from their national borders. Former 'Czechoslovak' locos have started operating in neighbouring countries as well, especially Poland and Hungary. This applies not only to modern loco designs, such as the Siemens 'Vectron' or Bombardier 'Traxx', but also to older locos operating cross-border and often deep into central Europe.

Metrans is one of the largest intermodal freight operators in central Europe, and while it is based in the Czech Republic, it is largely owned by the Hamburg Harbour Company, which is majority owned by Hamburg's city government. The Metrans fleet of silver-liveried locos has grown rapidly to around 80 with 40 Class 386 Bombardier 'Traxx' MS locos in service and, since late 2019, these have been joined by ten new Siemens 'Vectron' MS Class 383 locos. Metrans operates 18 terminals in multiple countries and had turnover of €450 million in 2020. Metrans 'Traxx' 386 021-0 passes through Kolín on 11 April 2018, with a northbound container train.

In the last ten years, the variety of freight locos to be seen in both the Czech Republic and Slovakia has increased with Polish-built Class ET41 Bo-Bo+Bo-Bo electrics (themselves derived from the PKP EU06 design, built in the UK in 1962–63), plus ET22 Co-Co locos regularly seen on the 3kV DC electrified parts of the networks. In this picture, PKP Cargo ET41 193 catches the late afternoon sun passing Choceň on 29 January 2015, with a westbound train of Polish coal.

ČD Cargo has operated profitably for many years, transporting around 65 million tonnes every year. Thanks to the pandemic, 2020 resulted in a loss of 276 million Czech Crowns (£9.3 million) and slightly lower traffic at 61 million tonnes. In better times, ČD Cargo loco 230 095-2 heads east at Bratislava hl.st, with a train of Polish chemical wagons, on 6 July 2018.

Former Romanian Railways (CFR) electric loco 430 109-5, now owned by logistics company, the Constantin Grup, is seen in Bratislava docks on 24 June 2012. These 25kV AC locos, which were built in Romania, historically never left the country, but are now used by freight operators into Hungary and as far as Kúty, on the Slovak border with the Czech Republic. Czech and Slovak engineering firms also overhaul them, which explains the ex-works paint on 430 109-5.

At Maťovce, on the eastern border of Slovakia with Ukraine, two ZSSK Cargo Class 125.8 double electric locos, led by 125 841-7, have just arrived on 5 July 2018, with an empty train of Ukrainian iron ore hoppers on the unique 1,520mm gauge ŠRT line, which reaches 87.1km into Slovakia from Užhorod in Ukraine. The ŠRT has continued to be used to import iron ore from Ukraine to the steelworks near Košice, which was privatised in the 1990s, and is now owned by American firm, US Steel. Plans were announced in 2008 to extend the 1,520mm gauge line from eastern Slovakia to Vienna but these made no real progress; Russia's annexation of parts of Ukraine in 2014 was, no doubt, a factor as relations between the two countries have largely broken down. The EU also opposed the project, as the new line would not have been standard gauge, and in mid-2021, the Austrian government announced it no longer supported the plan.

Velim – test centre for Europe

East of Prague, near the small towns of Velim and Cerhenice, is one of Europe's longest established rail testing circuits. The Velim test tracks are owned by ČD subsidiary, Výzkumný ústav železniční (VUZ – Railway Research Institute), which runs the test centre that was first built in 1963. It is used by multiple European train manufacturers to gain approval tests or mileage accumulation for new designs. There are two test circuits; the bigger one is 13.272km long, with a 230km/h speed limit for tilting trains, and the smaller one is 3.951km long.

Until 1989, the Velim test circuits were mainly used by Czechoslovak manufacturers, but by the mid-1990s, this had changed. A brand-new type SIE C651 metro EMU, built in Vienna by Siemens for Singapore, is seen at the test centre on 26 October 1995. Nineteen of these trains were delivered in the mid-1990s, and all are scheduled for replacement by 2024.

Many new trains for the UK have been tested at Velim since 2000. In 2018, two Class 68 locos (68019 and 68021) and a new CAF-built 'Nova3' push-pull set were being tested at the circuit. 68019 *Brutus* is seen between test runs. In the background, on the left, is a Škoda-built double-deck train for DB Regio in Germany.

Chapter 6
Competition flourishes

The Czech Republic was one of the first countries in Eastern Europe to open its rail network to private passenger operators. Initial small operations by new companies, often operating a single short line in the 1990s, have developed to the position where multiple contracts have been tendered and a wide variety of companies now run services alongside national operator, ČD. These contracts are organised both by regional governments and by the national transport ministry for cross-country routes that cross regional administrative borders. Contracts are normally awarded to the lowest cost operator, although some contracts require more modern trains to be provided as well. For passengers, the tendering system has added complexity, as on some routes, the new operators only accept their own tickets, although the Czech government is belatedly introducing a national ticketing system to remove these problems.

The Czech experience of open access inter-city competition is almost unique in Europe in that multiple operators compete on the same routes, both with each other as well as former monopolist ČD. All the Czech open access operators have expanded services across the border into Slovakia, and often much further afield, as well. Slovakia has seen less purely domestic competition, although some passenger services have been contracted to non-ZSSK operators.

Early competition was provided by new company, Viamont, which took over services on the Trutnov–Svoboda nad Úpou line in December 1997, using Class 810 railcars leased from ČD. Viamont-liveried 810 205-5 is seen at Trutnov on 30 August 2005, with train Os15724, the 13.45 to Svobada nad Úpou.

Early private operators

Newly established private operator, Viamont, took over operation of two regional railway lines and operated passenger trains on them in the late 1990s, starting with Trutnov–Svoboda nad Úpou in December 1997, and Sokolov–Kraslice from 1998. Services were operated with Class 810 railcars leased from ČD, although Class 704 and 742 locos were also used. Viamont later reopened the international route to Germany, closed in 1945, from Kraslice to Klingenthal (and onwards to Zwotental) in 2000 in co-operation with German operator, Vogtlandbahn, using German-built 'RegioSprinter' (German Class 654) DMUs. Viamont also operated the Karlovy Vary–Mariánské Lázně domestic route from 2006, with RegioSprinter units leased from Vogtlandbahn, which since 2011, has been owned by Italian state rail operator, Trenitalia.

Viamont subsequently won several more contracts and was renamed GW Train Regio in December 2011, as Viamont had already sold its rail freight subsidiary to OKD. In 2014, south Bohemian bus operator, ČSAD Jihotrans, bought GW Train Regio. Under its new name, GW Train Regio has continued to expand, taking over the Plzeň–Žatec–Chomutov–Most inter-regional service in December 2016, with a fleet of former German (DB) Class 628 DMUs. In 2017, the company also took over the operation of several lines serving the Šumava national park, to the southwest of České Budějovice.

A small section of the rail network in Moravia is owned by a municipal rail infrastructure manager, Železnice Desná (ŽD), with two branch lines totalling 22km from Šumperk to Kouty nad Desnou and the shorter branch to Sobotin. These have been owned by ŽD since ČD decided

GW Train Regio, ex-DB two-car DMU 628 329-5, complete with icicles, was recorded at Plzeň hl.n on 1 February 2017 before working a service to Most. On the left is ČD 'Regionova' DMU 914 089-8.

GW Train Regio Class 654 'RegioSprinter' DMU 654 012-3 is seen here in the operator's distinctive livery at Číčenice on 31 March 2019, with a service to Nový údolí, on the border with Germany.

Veolia-operated, ex-ČD 810 221-2 at Sobotin, on the Železnice Desná network, on 9 May 2009, on arrival with the 14.50 service from Šumperk. Since 2016, the short 3km Sobotin branch now only has summer weekend trains.

to otherwise close them following flooding in 1997. Services on the rebuilt line restarted in 2002, with French transport company, Veolia, operating them as Connex Morava, which was acquired by DB-owned Arriva in 2013.

Thanks to a CZK 418 million (£13.5 million) grant from the Czech government, ŽD electrified and modernised the 19km line from Šumperk to Kouty nad Desnou, with electric services starting in June 2016, these being initially operated by Arriva, but now by ČD, which won the tender for the line's operation. The short 3km Sobotin branch now only has summer weekend trains.

Arriva has expanded its Czech regional operations; in March 2016, it started operating open access services on weekdays from Prague to Benešov, around 50km south, these being aimed at commuters. These were not a financial success so were short-lived, much like a previous service in 2013, between Prague and Kralupy nad Vltavou.

However, Arriva Vlaky has since expanded its operations to include multiple inter-regional routes that it operates largely with ex-DB Class 628 DMUs (renumbered as Czech Class 845), although increasing numbers of 'Desiro Classic' DMUs (DB Class 642) are being used, which were also obtained from Germany. A three-year contract from December 2019 includes routes from Prague to Tanvald, Rakovnik and České Budějovice (via Písek), while a seven-year contract starting from December 2020 saw Arriva take over the R14 cross-country route from Pardubice to Liberec and Ústí nad Labem.

Following electrification, the Šumperk to Kouty nad Desnou line is served by both loco-hauled and EMU services. Class 162 electric loco 162 114-3, hired from Czech private operator, Regiojet, with special Arriva branding, and a single former DB Intercity coach are seen at Šumperk on the first day of electric services, 13 June 2016. Arriva only operated electric services on the line until December 2016, when ČD took over, and it only leased the Class 162 for part of that time.

Open access revolution

In 2011, a new privately owned open access operator called Regiojet began operation by running trains on the Prague–Ostrava route. Regiojet had been established by the largest Czech long distance bus operator, Student Agency. The new rail company used refurbished coaches bought from Western European operators and a fleet of nine Class 162 locos that had spent many years in Italy, after not being bought by ČSD in 1992. Both locos and trains were given a bright yellow livery that was based on the Student Agency bus livery and were highly distinctive as a result. Regiojet was successful in filling its trains, in part by using its existing long distance bus customer database to market its services and setting up ticket offices at every station it served.

A year later, in 2012, another new private operator began services on the same Prague–Ostrava route. Leo Express took a different approach, after buying five brand new 3kV DC 'Flirt' EMUs from Swiss manufacturer Stadler in 2010, by highlighting the Swiss quality of the brand-new trains in its launch advertising.

Within three years, the new operators had achieved around 55 per cent market share and prices paid by passengers had declined by nearly half. However, neither the new entrants nor ČD were making any profits, as they were trapped in a price war. ČD, then the dominant operator in the Czech Republic, was dropping its prices by almost 80 per cent in some cases, despite using new and expensive 'Pendolino' EMUs for almost all of its commercial services.

Within a decade, the new entrants and lower fares had doubled the number of rail passengers on the route, in part as Regiojet ceased operating its pre-existing parallel long distance bus services. Long running legal action by both Regiojet and Leo Express has resulted in the EU Commission finding that ČD unfairly cut its prices between 2011 and 2019, as it too was making a loss in the process. Exactly what compensation may be mandated for the private operators remained unclear in mid-2021, but it may be substantial.

Regiojet introduced its bold new livery in 2011, although for Czech passengers the colours were already synonymous with Regiojet's bus operator parent company, Student Agency. A Regiojet train from Košice to Prague, formed of former Austrian Railways (ÖBB) coaches, leaves Žilina on 7 November 2018, behind loco 162 113.

Regiojet has expanded its fleet by buying large numbers of second-hand coaches in Austria, Switzerland, and Germany. It has also acquired 'Traxx' locos built by Bombardier at Kassel in Germany, this plant changing to Alstom ownership in January 2021, following the acquisition of Bombardier. The first batch of four Class 386.2 'Traxx' MS2e locos were delivered in 2018. 386 203 is seen passing Vojkovice nad Svratkou, a few kilometres south of Brno, on the 160km/h Břeclav to Brno line, with a Praha hl.n to Vienna service on 1 April 2019.

Regiojet also hires in locomotives from freight companies and other passenger operators, including ČD on occasions, to cover for shortages in its own fleet. Arriva-owned and liveried veteran 'Bobina' loco, 140 079-5, was hired on several occasions in the summer of 2017. The loco is seen at Olomouc hl.n on 10 July 2017, with train IC1010, the 10.30 Havířov–Praha hl.n.

The Leo Express Class 480 'Flirt' fleet are intensively diagrammed and, pre-pandemic, could be seen in the Czech Republic, Slovakia, and Poland. The units all have a predominantly black livery and initially had gold stripes above the windows. Unit 480 002-5 is seen passing though Kolín at speed on 4 July 2013, when only around a year old, with a Prague to Bohumín service.

Arriva Vlaky started long distance open access services in 2016, between Prague and selected Slovak cities, and these share the Prague–Olomouc route with three other passenger competitors, making this section of railway the most competitive in terms of operator numbers of any main line route in the world! Arriva use DMUs sold to them by parent company, DB, in Germany with the former DB Class 628 two-car sets reclassified as Czech Class 845. Arriva Vlaky 845 001-7 arrives at Kolín on 11 April 2018, with a Nitra (Slovakia) to Prague service.

From March 2016, yet another operator started services on a core part of the same route when Arriva commenced weekend services aimed at students on the Prague–Olomouc–Uherské Hradiště–Trenčín (Slovakia) line. These services operated using ex-DB Class 628 DMUs and were later expanded from September 2018, to operate daily between Prague and Nitra via Trenčín. This meant that there were sometimes four competing trains each hour on the Prague to Olomouc section of the route.

Expansion internationally

Both Regiojet and Leo Express introduced services from Prague to Žilina and Košice, in Slovakia, by extending existing services to Ostrava. Regiojet expanded rapidly by adding Slovak domestic services between Bratislava, Žilina and Košice in December 2014, but ended these as the Slovak government decided to give students and pensioners free travel on the competing state-owned ZSSK trains (the government paid ZSSK) and refused to allow Regiojet to be included in the free travel subsidy scheme.

Regiojet introduced services on the second busiest Czech domestic route, between Prague and Brno in December 2016, extending most trains to Bratislava. Regiojet has continued to invest in refurbished rolling stock, both daytime inter-city and overnight sleeper/couchette cars. It has also expanded its loco fleet with the leasing of Siemens 'Vectron' MS locos, mainly, but not exclusively, from European Loco Leasing (ELL), and has also bought four Bombardier (now Alstom) 'Traxx' MS2e/Class 386.2 locos. Also on order are 15 newer Class 388.2 'Traxx 3' locos, the first of which were delivered in 2020.

In December 2017, Regiojet started services to Vienna via Brno and, in July 2020, extended some Vienna services to Budapest, although initially these only ran until September, because of pandemic border closures. A new service to Kraków and Przemyśl, Poland, was due to start in March 2021, having been delayed by regulatory approvals; however, this was then postponed until later in the year. The new services had a difficult start as the Coronavirus pandemic led to restrictions on movement and all the open access operators cut back their services significantly, although in summer 2020, with little time to prepare, Regiojet introduced a new overnight service from Prague to Rijeka, Croatia, for holiday makers. This service was so successful that it was expanded in 2021 to a longer train serving both Rijeka and Split on the Adriatic coast.

Not every open access route has succeeded. In December 2014, Regiojet began Bratislava–Košice services wholly within Slovakia, but passenger numbers were relatively low, owing to the Slovak government's generous free travel scheme, which gives students and pensioners free travel, but only on ZSSK's trains. As access to this scheme was not available to other commercial operators, Regiojet withdrew its last Bratislava–Košice service on 31 January 2017. Regiojet used its fleet of Siemens 'Vectron' MS locos for the services, with 193 206 pictured here at Trnava, between Bratislava and Žilina, with a train to Košice on 3 February 2015, shortly after the services were introduced.

New trains and owner for Leo Express

Before the pandemic, Leo Express had expanded its services into Poland by operating to Kraków and had announced plans to run to the Ukrainian border at Medyka, although these services did not start in 2020. Leo Express briefly operated open access services in Germany, both on its own by taking over the defunct Locomore business in 2017, and later, from 2018, as a sub-contractor to Flixtrain, although this ceased in early 2020.

Leo Express had also agreed a contract for up to 33 new EMUs to be built in China by rolling stock manufacturer, CRRC. Introduction of these trains, designated Class 665 and to be known as 'Sirius', was initially due in 2019, but was delayed by the pandemic, with only the first two 3kV DC/25kV AC trains arriving for testing at the Velim test centre by mid-2021. In late 2020, Leo Express announced it was planning to modify the order for additional trains to also operate from 15kV AC, as used in Germany and Austria.

Leo Express had a 2019 turnover of 1.1 billion Czech Crowns (£36 million) and profits of 150 million Crowns (£4.9 million). In 2021, it was confirmed that Spanish national rail operator RENFE was planning to buy a 50 per cent stake in Leo Express; previously, a possible sale to Czech national rail operator, ČD, was discussed by senior politicians in 2020, but did not proceed. In 2020 and early 2021, Leo Express was loss making because of the pandemic-related suspension of most of its activities.

The first Class 665 'Sirius' EMU built by CRRC at Zhuzhou, China, on test at the Velim test track in the Czech Republic on 21 November 2020. (Leo Express)

Open access operators take on contracted services

While Arriva Vlaky began operating contracted services, before introducing short distance and then international open access services, both the Czech open access pioneers Regiojet and Leo Express have also won operating contracts that replaced ČD.

Regiojet first expanded into regional services with its first Czech contract beginning in December 2018, around Ústí nad Labem, this initially using second-hand Class 628 DMUs from Germany, although seven brand new 'Elf II' EMUs are on order from Polish manufacturer, Pesa, for delivery from 2022 to replace the DMUs. From December 2019, the company took over the R8 Brno–Bohumín inter-regional route with an eight-year contract, this initially using modern leased 'Vectron' MS locos and refurbished coaches acquired second-hand from Swiss Railways (SBB) and Austrian Railways (ÖBB). In mid-April 2021, it was announced that Regiojet will take over the 135km R23 cross-country route between Kolín and Ústí nad Labem using refurbished loco-hauled trains.

In Slovakia, Regiojet had a nine-year contract, which expired in late 2020, to operate trains on the Bratislava–Dunajská Streda–Komárno line, using a mixture of former German Class 643 'Talent' and Class 628 (ex-DB) DMUs, plus some loco-hauled trains. A new two-year contract was awarded to a consortium of ZSSK with Austrian Railways (ÖBB) in 2020.

Leo Express has also obtained a regional concession contract in the Czech Republic, starting a ten-year contract for services centred on Ústí nad Orlicí in December 2019, using a fleet of leased Alstom 'Lint' DMUs, previously employed in Germany.

For services around Ústí nad Labem, Regiojet has given its ex-DB Class 628 DMUs a green livery, specified by the regional government. 928 310-1 is seen leading a service to Most at Ústí nad Labem hl.n on the first day of Regiojet operation on 15 December 2019. These DMUs are due to be replaced in 2022 by new Pesa-built 'Elf II' EMUs.

From December 2019, Regiojet took over the R8 Brno–Bohumín inter-regional route, initially using modern leased 'Vectron' MS locos. One of the more unusual hires was EP Cargo-liveried and Slovakian-registered loco 383 062-7, which was recorded approaching Hranice na Moravě on 17 December 2019, with a R8 Brno to Bohumín service.

Regiojet intends to replace the leased 'Vectron' locos on the R8 contract and its international routes with its new fleet of 'Traxx 3' locos. The first of these in service was 388 202, seen on its first day in traffic at Brno hl.n on 23 December 2020, with train RJ1121, the 14.44 Brno Kralove Pole to Bohumín. (Shaun Wallace)

Regiojet began its contract in Slovakia to operate services on the Bratislava–Dunajská Streda–Komárno line on 4 March 2012. Initially, a fleet of ten-year old German Class 643 'Talent' DMUs were leased and eventually all received Regiojet's familiar yellow livery. Still in the red, white, and blue of the Prignitzer Eisenbahn (PEG), 643 368-2 is seen leaving Bratislava hl.st on 28 June 2012, with the 10.42 Regiojet service to Dunajská Streda.

Following accident damage to several of the 'Talent' DMUs, Regiojet introduced some limited loco-hauled services on the Bratislava to Komárno route, using Class 749 or 750 diesels hired from other operators. In early 2017, 750 096-0 was hired from Czech freight operator, KDS. It is seen in this picture reversing empty stock at Bratislava hl.st, prior to working a train to Komárno. Towards the end of Regiojet's contract for services on this line, it also used 'Eurorunner' Class 223 diesel locos leased from Beacon with ex-German double-deck coaches.

Chapter 7

International connections enhanced

As landlocked countries surrounded by neighbours, also with dense railway networks, the Czech Republic and Slovakia between them have multiple railway lines that cross borders, although some lines, especially with Germany and Austria, closed in 1945, in the aftermath of World War Two. The division of Czechoslovakia in 1993 created more new international border crossings with the railways that went between the two countries as well.

In 1989, Czechoslovakia had limited connections with Western Europe, with a handful of long distance services, mainly serving Vienna, but much better services to fellow Eastern Bloc countries, with through trains to East Berlin and Budapest. Even in the early 1990s, the Czech spa town of Karlovy Vary had through sleeping cars from countries as far away as Russia and Bulgaria; those from Russia continuing well into the 21st century.

In 2021, both Prague and Bratislava are well served by regular international express 'Eurocity' services, operated by ČD and ZSSK, in conjunction with neighbouring countries, and also by the three different open access operators. 'Eurocity' services also connect Warsaw and Kraków with Ostrava and Prague and, via the Czech Republic, both Bratislava and Vienna.

ČD has invested in modern locomotives and rolling stock for the most important services and, since 2014, has operated Siemens-built 'Railjet' push-pull trains on the Prague–Vienna route, with most trains extended south to Graz. In late 2017, ČD leased ten Siemens 'Vectron' Class 193 locos for the 'Eurocity' routes from Prague to Budapest and Berlin, some of which operate as far north as Kiel and Hamburg, with the ČD locos. ZSSK has also leased 'Vectron' locos and operates these to Vienna, as well as internally in Slovakia.

Until the arrival of the Czech Class 380 locos from around 2010 onwards, and the Railjet trains from 2014, ZSSK Class 350 dual voltage locos were used for most main international trains on the Prague to Bratislava (and onwards to Budapest) route, as well as key domestic trains in Slovakia. In a relatively short lived early red and white livery, 350 001-4 arrives at Břeclav on 13 September 2009, with a Prague–Budapest 'Eurocity' service formed almost entirely of ČD stock, in the orange and white livery then used for international coaches. 350 001-4 now carries a retro livery based on its original 1973 livery.

Small batches of Polish locos, owned by PKP Intercity, are equipped with Czech signalling systems, and can be seen working as far west as Prague. In recent years, the earlier PKP IC Class EU07 locos have not reached further than Bohumín, although previously they went to Prague daily, and even worked domestic trains in the Czech Republic. PKP IC Class EP09 locos do still regularly work beyond Bohumín. EP09 028 is seen approaching Kolín on 11 April 2018, with EC114 from Kraków to Prague. The train is entirely formed of ČD stock, in the latest white and blue liveries.

ČD used its new 'Pendolino' EMUs to work EC services to Vienna from 2006 until 2012. These services are now operated using the 'Railjet' push-pull sets and Class 1216 locomotives, with most services extended south in Austria to Graz. ČD 681 003-0 arrives in Vienna on 7 May 2009, at the former Wien Südbahnhof terminus, which closed in December that year, and has been replaced by the nearby new Wien Hauptbahnhof.

Until December 2017, the 160km/h Class 371 dual voltage (3kV DC/15kV AC) locos worked most international express trains between Prague and Dresden. In the early 2000s, they were also used by German operator, DB, for Berlin–Warsaw trains as far as Rzepin, Poland. In a one-off livery based on the Czech flag, 371 201-5 pauses at Ústí nad Labem on 3 April 2016 with train EC173, the 06.36 Hamburg Altona–Budapest Keleti. This loco started life as a German loco (DR 230 001, DB 180 001) and was given to ČD in 2003, as compensation for an accident that severely damaged one of its dual voltage Class 372 locos.

With electrification of the line across the Austrian border in Summerau, international trains were introduced between Linz and Prague. Austrian 'Taurus' Eurosprinter loco 1116 253-4 is seen arriving at České Budějovice, with EC100, the 14.22 Salzburg to Prague, on 13 May 2009. Immediately behind the loco is a Czech sleeping coach, which presumably was empty at mid-afternoon, unless it was very late! Evening and morning trains on this route are still used to convey Prague–Zürich sleeping cars as far as Linz, where they are added to Vienna–Zürich overnight trains.

Regional cross-border services expand

In 1990, regional cross-border connections with Austria and Germany mainly consisted of trains that ran to the border, where passengers changed from ČSD to the other country's train, with few through workings, although there were some to what had been East Germany. Slovakia has multiple cross-border rail connections with Hungary, most having been built when the country was part of Hungary before World War One. Usage of these connections by passenger services declined from the 1990s, and several no longer have passenger services, although they are still used by freight. Several electrified connections between Slovakia and Hungary exist, and most international passenger and freight traffic is concentrated on these.

There are several cross-border lines into Poland from both the Czech Republic and Slovakia. Some are only used by freight trains, having lost their regional train connections in the last 30 years, while others have regular passenger services, mostly international long-distance services. The line from Čierna nad Tisou to Chop is the only standard gauge line connecting Slovakia to Ukraine. There is also a short section of 1,520mm line there to the yards at Dobra, just inside Slovakia, although the freight-only ŠRT 1,520mm line (see Chapter 5) also connects the two countries.

21st century expansion

The entry of both the Czech Republic and Slovakia into the EU in 2004, and their subsequent membership of the 'Schengen' travel area from 2007, led to a substantial increase in regional passenger services, especially with Austria and Germany. In some cases, lines closed as long ago as May 1945 were rebuilt and reopened, while in other cases, little used lines were modernised with new trains and frequent cross-border services introduced. Journeys that in 1989 would have required visas and complex international tickets became commuter routes as cross-border commuting became normality. Many Slovaks now work in Austria, earning Austrian wages while living at lower Slovak costs. In the Vienna area, the Kittsee to Bratislava–Petržalka line reopened, with Austrian 15kV AC electrification into the Slovakian station in 1998; the other main Bratislava to Vienna line via Marchegg is now being electrified, with work due to be complete by the end of 2023.

Prior to 1989, there were limited regional services between Czechoslovakia and East Germany, despite both being communist states. ČSD ran services from Rumburk via East German territory as 'corridor trains' to Liberec and these called at Zittau, where border facilities were built on the platforms for any passengers getting on or off. Not long before East Germany ceased to exist, ČSD 810 470-5, complete with recently painted out red star, and an older trailer, arrive at Zittau, with a train to Liberec on 13 April 1990.

Within a few years, regular cross-border services connecting Liberec with German cities were introduced. From 2002, French-owned company, Connex, operated trains branded as 'Lausitzbahn', connecting Liberec and Germany as part of a contract it had in Saxony. For a period in 2004–05, there was even a through 'Interconnex' service between Liberec and Berlin, operated like all the other services, using then modern Siemens 'Desiro' DMUs. On 24 July 2006, Connex 'Desiro' VT562 is seen in Liberec with a train to Cottbus, alongside ČD 810 324-4. At far left is a DB Regio Class 612 DMU from Dresden.

In Slovakia, several cross-border railways to Hungary lost their already limited passenger services after 2002 as, with low population density on both sides of the border along with rising car ownership, passenger numbers fell. This picture at Lenartovce on 1 June 2007 shows a fairly rare sight; the units were both built at the same Czech factory in Studénka, but belong to different railways, and are rarely seen together. On the left is ZSSK 810 604-9, and on the right, the Hungarian version Bzmot 247, which has just arrived from Bánréve, over the border in Hungary. The limited international service on this line ended in December 2009.

The town of Slovenské Nové Mesto (Slovak New Town) came into existence in 1920, as the rest of the town of Sátoraljaújhely was now in Hungary, thanks to the new borders for Czechoslovakia, which ensured the Košice to Chop line was entirely in the new country. Passenger services connecting the two ended in December 2008, although the railway remains open for freight trains. Not long before passenger services ended, MAV diesel loco M41 2306 is pictured at Slovenské Nové Mesto on 24 April 2006, with the 11.15 service to the Hungarian city of Miskolc.

The hourly service from Bratislava to Vienna is the last diesel-hauled service between capital cities in the EU and, from 2024, will be electric powered under current plans. Trains are operated using ÖBB Class 2016 'Eurorunner' diesel locos and push-pull sets than normally include at least one ZSSK coach. In the picture, 2016 025-6 is seen at Bratislava hl.st, with a train for Vienna on 4 February 2015. ZSSK provided Class 750/754 locos, alongside ÖBB Class 2143, for these services when they first began operating as regular through trains in 2004, after Slovakia joined the EU. Previously, passengers normally needed to change trains at the border station in Marchegg and clear immigration checks.

In the northeast corner of Slovakia, there is a connection to Polish railways on the line from Medzilaborce, Slovakia, and Łupków, Poland, which crosses the border in the 416-metre long Łupków Tunnel, built under the Carpathian Mountains. Strategically important when it was built in the 19th century, and severely damaged in World War Two, it has mainly been used by freight trains, although a limited passenger service ran until 2010. Since 2017, trains have run again at weekends in the summer. Before regular passenger services ended, ZSSK railcar 810 380 and PKP Cargo diesel ST43 345 are seen together at Łupków on 15 August 2008.

Having multiple borders means that countries like Slovakia often provide motive power into their neighbours' territory, for example, ZSSK Class 350 locos operated to Budapest for many years. To balance such workings, neighbouring railways often provide their locos for domestic use abroad, and such arrangements between ZSSK and MAV, in Hungary, have led to MAV locos working entirely domestic services for ZSSK. Such arrangements are rarely permanent, but may last a year or two, until the mileage balance is equalised. In 2015, there were several domestic Slovak trains booked for MAV Class V43/431 electric locos, some took them north of Bratislava. MAV 431 014 is seen at Leopoldov on 3 February 2015, after arriving from the Slovak capital.

Between the Czech Republic and Germany, multiple lines have reopened since the 1990s, some involving reinstatement of track lifted or left derelict since 1945. In the early 1990s, the first experimental cross-border services ran on some lines linking Saxony with Bohemia. The first cross-border passenger train since 1945, on the line from Karlovy Vary to Aue via Johanngeorgenstadt, crossed the border into Germany on 17 April 1992, and regular services were reinstated later that year. In 1993, services ran on the line connecting Chemnitz and Cranzahl, in Germany, with Vejprty and the line to Chomutov but, despite being one of the first to reopen, this line has suffered from repeated closure threats, with only summer weekend trains planned in 2021.

In 2000, the Kraslice–Zwotental (Saxony) line reopened with Czech private operator, Viamont, running the trains in conjunction with German company, Vogtlandbahn. Two further reopening projects, both of which involved lines being rebuilt, have come to fruition in recent years. On 4 July 2014, the short Sebnitz–Dolní Poustevna line, southeast of Dresden, reopened. Reinstatement of around a kilometre of line took nearly a decade, thanks to multiple political delays. Passengers from the region around Dolní Poustevna can now reach the main Czech regional town, Děčín, on direct trains operated by DB Regio using Class 642 'Desiro' DMUs, via Germany in around an hour, which is less than half the previous travel time wholly within the Czech Republic.

At the western end of the Czech Republic, the line from Selb–Plössberg, in Bavaria, reopened to Aš in the Czech Republic in December 2015, after a €25 million rebuilding project. The German private operator, Oberpfalzbahn, was contracted to run trains using modern DMUs between Marktredwitz (on the cross-border route via Schirdning that remained open after 1945) to Hof via the Czech cities of Cheb and Aš. Reopening a further line connecting Germany and the Czech Republic between Holzhau (Saxony) and Moldava v Krušných has been under discussion for over a decade and in 2020 gained official support from both the Czech and German authorities, although a firm timescale has yet to be agreed.

The reopened line from Karlovy Vary to the German border at Johanngeorgenstadt was operated using both DMUs and loco-hauled trains. ČD diesel 742 195-1 is seen just after arrival in Germany at Johanngeorgenstadt on 2 December 2011.

Chapter 8

Narrow gauge mixed fortunes

In 1989, ČSD operated several narrow-gauge systems in what would become both the Czech Republic and Slovakia. The vast majority were the remnants of once bigger systems built before World War One, but the metre gauge Strub rack-equipped line from Štrba to Štrbské Pleso, in the Tatra mountains in Slovakia, was more modern. This opened after complete rebuilding in 1970 and using Swiss-built EMUs for the Nordic World Ski Championships, which were held at Štrbské Pleso that year. The original Riggenbach rack-equipped line from Štrba to Štrbské Pleso dating from 1896 had closed in 1932 and been dismantled in the 1940s.

Over the three decades since 1989, some of the former ČSD narrow gauge lines have been privatised or closed, while others that had their lost passenger services or closed completely before 1989 have reopened as heritage railways. Several lines, including the entire Tatra system in Slovakia, remain in the ownership of the relevant national rail operator.

Slovakia electrified narrow gauge

The electrified 29km metre gauge network serving resorts in the High Tatra mountains, Tatranská elektrická železnica (TEŽ), opened in stages between 1908 and 1912, with electric operation from the start. The original four-axle tram-derived vehicles were replaced in 1969 by 18 new lightweight units built by ČKD Tatra and based on the successful Tatra T2/T3 bogie tram design. These, designated ČSD EMU 89.0 series and later Class 420.95, were replaced from 2000 by new Class 425.95 EMUs based on the Stadler GTW2/6 design, which were assembled mainly in Slovakia, with parts from Stadler and Adtranz.

The historic TEŽ terminus at Poprad Tatry was alongside the main station on the south side of the main line. The TEŽ line went under the main line and then headed north. From mid-1991, the new high-level TEŽ station replaced this with a new connection to the old TEŽ route. ČKD Tatra-built EMU 420 968-0 is seen at the original Poprad Tatry station on 4 April 1991. The new high-level station opened later in 1991.

Within a decade, the old tram-derived units were replaced by Stadler-built trains, based on those used by Swiss metre gauge operators. One of these, ZSSK 425 963-6, is seen climbing towards Štrbské Pleso on 9 April 2012. (Shaun Wallace)

A view of the new high-level station at Poprad Tatry with unit 425 906-2 awaiting departure on 15 September 2004. The connection used by empty trains to the TEŽ depot can be seen curving under the viaduct, this diverges just before the station, as the depot is alongside the Žilina–Košice main line.

Five new rack-equipped EMUs from Stadler entered service from August 2021 to replace the existing Class 405.95 trains on the Štrba to Štrbské Pleso line. In the picture above, the Tatra mountains provide a backdrop for 405 953-1, one of the 1969-built trains, at Štrbské Pleso on 9 April 2012, with the 12.02 service to Štrba. The five new Class 495.95 trains, which are derived from similar ABeh 2/6 units for the Swiss company, MVR (Transports Montreux-Vevey-Riviera), are named after the Tatra mountain peaks, and will be able to operate on the rest of the TEŽ network as well. In the lower picture, brand new 495 951-6 *Bradvica* is seen on test on 29 March 2021. A Stadler two-axle electro-diesel rack-fitted locomotive, numbered as 485 951-4, has also been supplied. Based on similar Swiss HGem 2/2 types, this is for maintenance and snow clearing duties. Two historic trains have been retained on the TEŽ system, although these are no longer ZSSK owned; a Ganz-built train, dating from the line's opening, and a ČKD Tatra Class 420.95. (Shaun Wallace/ZSSK)

West of the Tatras, the short 5.4km 600VDC Trenčianska Teplá–Trenčianske Teplice (Trenčianska Elektrická Železnic) 760mm gauge line was operated by ZSSK until 2011, when regular services ended. It has been run as a tourist railway since then. The three trains had a unique blue and cream livery in ZSSK days, 411 903-8 being recorded at Trenčianska Teplá on 14 September 2004, waiting to leave with the 15.05 service to Trenčianske Teplice.

The 760mm gauge line connecting the spa town of Trenčianske Teplice with Trenčianska Teplá, on the Bratislava to Žilina main line, opened as an electric railway on 27 June 1909. The ZSSK Class 411 EMUs used date from 1951 and were delivered as the ČSD EMU 46.0 series; they were rebuilt in the mid-1980s. The line largely runs alongside the road connecting the two towns. 411 903-8 is approaching Trenčianska Teplá on 14 September 2004, with the 14.38 from Trenčianske Teplice.

Heritage variety in Slovakia

East of Banská Bystrica, the former 760mm gauge forestry railway, Čiernohronská železnica (Čiernohronská Railway or ČHŽ), connecting the town of Čierny Balog with the standard gauge main line from Banská Bystrica to Margecany closed completely in 1982, but was declared a national monument by the government, although no funds were available for the line. Volunteers began the process of rebuilding and reopening the line, and services on part of the route restarted in 1992.

Since then, the line, which is famous for crossing the town's football pitch in Čierny Balog (with trains sometimes interrupting games), has been extended further. Plans to convert the line from the current tourist operation to year-round public transport have been announced and in 2020, the EMU fleet of the Waldenburgerbahn 750mm gauge line near Basel, Switzerland, (which is being rebuilt for metre gauge operation) was bought and moved to Slovakia in May 2021. The seven type BDe 4/4 two-car units and ten type Bt trailers were moved to Hronec, initially by barge from Basel to Bratislava, and then by rail. Assuming funding is found, the line will be modernised and electrified by the mid-2020s.

Several more 'heritage' narrow gauge lines exist in Slovakia; the main ones are the former 'pioneer railway' in Košice, and two former forestry railways, one in Nitra (at the Slovak Agricultural Museum) and the other the Kysucko–Orava Forest Railway, which preserves a line built with zig-zag switchbacks at the Museum of the Kysuce Village (Skanzen Vychylovka), north and east of Čadca and Žilina.

The metre gauge 'pioneer railway' in the western suburbs of Košice was built in 1955 to train future railway employees. Several other similar lines were built in Czechoslovakia in the 1950s, including in the Czech cities of Prešov and Plzeň, but these have since closed. Following threats to close the line in the 1990s, it has been funded by Košice city council since 2003, with rolling stock maintained by a charitable trust.

The current Čiernohronská železnica heritage operation uses both steam and diesel locomotives. On 30 April 2012, ČHŽ Number 3 (0-6-0T, built ČKD 1948/2209) leaves Čierny Balog with an empty stock train. (Shaun Wallace)

The most recent extension of the ČHŽ line is the short Čierny Balog to Dobroč branch, which reopened on 30 April 2012. The first public train is seen being propelled out of Dobroč on the opening day by Hungarian-built diesel loco TU45 001, which was delivered to the ČHŽ when new in 1961. (Shaun Wallace)

The 4.2km Košice Children's Heritage Railway (Košická detská historická železnica – KDHŽ) line operates during the summer. KDHŽ has two steam locos and three ČKD T 211.0-design diesel shunters numbered as Class TU29, which are also allocated full ZSSK computer numbers as Class 701.9. Almost all the rolling stock used is over 100 years old, although some of it has been rebuilt more than once! TU29 2003 is seen at the Alpinka terminus, at the western end of the line, with a train for Čermeľ on 4 July 2018.

Czech Republic – uncertain future for biggest system

There are several narrow-gauge lines in the Czech Republic, almost all use 760mm gauge track, which reflects their history as being built by Austrian companies prior to World War One. Two systems still have daily passenger trains in 2021, but rely on diesel traction and, in many cases, locomotives that date from the late-1950s. Unlike the situation in Slovakia, where new trains and/or electrification is planned for the main routes, there are threats to the long-term future of both major Czech systems.

The largest narrow-gauge system still in operation in the Czech Republic is centred on Jindřichův Hradec. The 79km 760mm gauge system was opened between 1897 and 1910, and, after threats of closure in the 1970s and again after 1989, it was sold for a symbolic one crown in 1997 to Jindřichohradecké místní dráhy (JHMD), which had been formed by local residents and rail enthusiasts to promote the future of the lines. JHMD agreed to rent the lines from ČD. The southern line to Nová Bystřice was quickly reopened in July 1997 (ČD had shut it in January 1997) and from 23 October 1997, JHMD also took over operation of services on the northern part of the network to Obrataň, using the former ČD rolling stock.

Services are operated by a mixture of ex-ČSD Class 705 diesel locos, dating from 1954–58, and modernised MBxd2 diesel railcars, originally built for Polish state railway, PKP. Steam locos acquired from Poland and Romania are used for some tourist services.

The contract JHMD has with regional governments ends in October 2024, and the replacement of train services with buses for all or part of the network was under discussion in mid-2021. The regional governments also want newer rolling stock to be used for any future contract, although without a long-term contract this is unlikely to be acquired.

Diesel loco T47 019/705 919, still in ČSD livery, is seen alongside Romanian-built 0-8-0T steam loco U46 001 at Jindřichův Hradec on 9 July 2004. The steam loco was working a scheduled service to Nová Bystřice.

The ČSD T47/Class 705 was built by ČKD between 1954 and 1959. Twenty-one were delivered to ČSD, which also used them on the now closed 750mm gauge system at Frýdlant v Čechách, near Ostrava, and the 760mm line in Ružomberok, which closed in 1974. Forty-five similar 750mm gauge locos were sold to the Soviet Union and numbered as ТУ3 001 to 045. Since 1997, JHMD has rebuilt some of its locos with new engines and sold one (705 921) to a Russian narrow-gauge line. Both carrying new and different liveries, two of the JHMD locos, 705 911, on the left, and 705 915, on jacks on the right, are pictured outside the depot at Jindřichův Hradec on 9 July 2004.

The JHMD line shares a section of the electrified main line north of Jindřichův Hradec station. On 14 April 2004, T47 019/705 919 is seen approaching Jindřichův Hradec on the dual gauge section, with a single coach forming the 12.18 from Kamenice nad Lipou.

JHMD has now given every loco a unique livery. One of the original six prototype locos, T47 005/705 905 now has a green livery, as seen leaving Černovice u Tábora on 3 July 2014.

Still wholly operated by ČD, the shorter 20.2km line from Tremešná ve Slezsku to Osoblaha, west of Ostrava and just south of the Polish border, is normally operated using one Class 705 loco and a single coach. In the picture, 705 913 has just arrived at Osoblaha on 27 July 2004, with the 18.12 from Tremešná ve Slezsku. Steam and tourist trains are also operated by heritage groups during the summer months. After several months in 2020 where buses replaced trains owing to there being no available locomotive, plans to renovate several of the line's stations and overhaul at least one diesel locomotive were announced in 2021, meaning that rail services should resume later that year.

Czech tourist lines multiply

Several narrow-gauge heritage lines have been rebuilt or opened for tourist use in the last 30 years. At the Czech national railway museum in Lužná u Rakovníka, there is a short 800mm gauge line. Multiple other lines, which range from miniature railways in retail parks to recreated industrial lines, also now exist.

West of Brno, part of a mineral railway, built from Zastávka u Brna to coal mines in Zbýšov in 1862, has been converted from standard to 600mm gauge. Steam or diesel-hauled services operate on most summer Saturdays on the 2.7km long line. Henschel-built 0-4-0T No. 12311 is seen at Babice u Rosic, with the 11.05 Zastávka u Brna to Zbýšov Důl Jindřich. (Shaun Wallace)

Near Kolín, east of Prague, the former narrow-gauge railway has been partly rebuilt as a tourist attraction since 2000. The original line was 700mm gauge and designed specifically to transport sugar beet to the sugar factory in Kolín. It opened in April 1897 and closed in 1964, being demolished within a year. The reinstated heritage line is 600mm gauge and the first section opened in June 2007. The 4.5km long line has now been extended in stages as far as Býchory from 1 May 2015 and is normally steam operated. Later in 2015, diesel-electric loco BNE 50 is seen at Kolín–Sendražice on 9 August. This was also one of the hottest days that summer (39.5 degrees Celsius) so steam operation was banned and diesels had to substitute.

Chapter 9

Rail preservation large and small

Both the Czech Republic and Slovakia have extensive and active railway preservation activities, ranging from preservation by the state railway companies through to volunteer run societies. For relatively small countries, both outperform many bigger Western European countries, in terms of the amount and variety of rolling stock preserved and in using it regularly, other than during the Coronavirus pandemic! Most activities are aimed at, and priced for, the general public, rather than just rail enthusiasts. Steam-hauled special trains are regularly operated across both countries for anniversaries of individual lines; in fact, reduced track access charges apply to encourage such commemorative trains!

In the Czech Republic, ČD has been a major corporate sponsor of restoration activity, returning long derelict steam and diesel locos or trains to operational condition. This continues a tradition dating back to ČSD days when steam locos were retained for occasional use and, until the early 1990s, advertised in the public timetable when operating scheduled services in place of diesels! In normal years, multiple special trains with vintage locomotives operate in the Czech Republic, some operated by ČD, and others by private companies or chartered for groups.

ČD also operates the Czech national railway museum in Lužná u Rakovníka, west of Prague. A larger annex in Chomutov, with many stored locos, in the north of the country, plus a smaller one in Olomouc, are occasionally opened to the public. The National Technical Museum in Prague has a huge collection, much of it stored in Chomutov, but has developed plans to build a new railway museum on the site of the former ČD depot at Prague Masarykovo station, although exactly when this will happen is unclear.

ČSD maintained several main line steam locos and used them into the early 1990s, instead of diesels on a pre-planned basis, as well as for special or chartered trains. Škoda built 42 of this magnificent three-cylinder 4-8-2 design immediately after World War Two in 1946–47. 498 022 is one of two that survived and ČSD used it for special trains, seen here on 15 April 1990, being serviced at Mladá Boleslav, while working a special train.

ČD normally runs a programme of 'Nostalgia' trains, especially from Prague. Typical of the type of train is this view of 1928-built 2-6-2T 423 094 crossing the viaduct at Praha Žvahov on the steeply graded 'Prague Semmering' line, with a special train on 28 October 1995.

Both the Czech and Slovak national collections contain a wide variety of diesel locos, many in working order. Part of the Slovak collection, T444 0060 is seen at Bratislava Vychod depot on 24 June 2012. It is one of 174 locos (113 for ČSD, remainder for industrial users) mostly built by TSM in Martin, Slovakia, on behalf of ČKD, and later classified as Class 725.

More than 20 other heritage operations exist around the Czech Republic; some of these are restored or rebuilt narrow gauge lines while others use either the national SŽ network or branch lines that are no longer part of the national network. Volunteer rail enthusiast society Klub železničních cestovatelů (KŽC – Railway Travellers Club) has become both a major owner of preserved rolling stock and an operator of passenger trains.

KŽC operates summer weekend services on the main line network with vintage diesel locos or multiple units and has won small operating contracts for subsidised local passenger services. In addition to all this, KŽC runs several rail tours each year, aimed at its members, both in the Czech Republic and neighbouring countries.

In Slovakia, most of the national railway museum collection is kept at Bratislava Vychod depot, which is an operational depot. However, public access is possible and at least once a year (normally mid-June), a major public event takes place with the whole site open and multiple special and shuttle trains. Other items from the national collection are stored at Vrútky, in the centre of the country, and again the site is open occasionally. The Slovak national technical museum located alongside Bratislava hl.st station has a smaller collection of preserved locomotives and is normally open year-round. There are less 'heritage' operations in Slovakia, although enthusiast groups in Vrútky, Košice and other cities do arrange special trains with steam, diesel, and electric traction.

As well as locomotives, KŽC has a fleet of ex-ČSD Class 810 railcars and uses these for some public services, plus excursions, sometimes to neighbouring countries. A three-car set led by M152 0517 is seen at the end of the now closed Žacléř branch on 9 April 2017.

A preservation group, based at Vrútky depot in central Slovakia, arranges excursions using heritage stock. One of the few ex-ČSD 'M62' Class 781 locos in working order is sometimes used. In original livery as T679 1168 (781 168), the loco is seen near Strečno, between Žilina and Vrútky, with a charter train on 17 October 2010. Strečno Castle, dating back to the 14th century, is in the background.

Only one Class 776/T678 loco survived into preservation, T678 0012 (776 012). Class 775 loco T678 0012 (775 012) is still approved for main line operation. The loco has been restored to the orange livery carried when new and is seen at Sereď on 24 June 2012, with a special train from Bratislava to Zvolen, where it is based.

There are several minor lines that have heritage services, often only at weekends. The steeply graded 6km line from Velké Březno to Zubrnice was declared a museum railway in 1988, ten years after it closed, although it took until 2010 for museum operation on the whole line to begin. A 4.5km extension from Zubrnice to Lovečkovice is planned and partly built. Unusually, trains currently start on the national network at Ústí nad Labem-Střekov (and are integrated within the public transport fares for the Ústí area) and use the main line for 8.5km; this may end soon, as the line will be rebuilt with ETCS cab signalling. Trains are operated using vintage railcars dating from 1950, and occasionally locomotives. Ex-ČSD railcar M131 1280 is seen at the end of the line at Zubrnice on 3 April 2016.

ČD maintains some steam locos away from Prague or the museum at Lužná u Rakovníka. Built in 1947, 4-8-2 475 101 is used for occasional steam specials on the main line and based in Brno, at Brno Maloměřice depot. The loco is seen at Brno hl.n on 9 May 2009.

Chapter 10
High speed future

In 2021, the maximum speed of any train in either the Czech Republic or Slovakia was 160km/h, but changes are planned, especially in the Czech Republic, where the government has announced ambitious plans to develop a high-speed rail network in the country over the next three decades. This will also link to planned high-speed connections in neighbouring countries. In Slovakia, a decade long programme of rebuilding existing lines has resulted in lengthy sections of high quality 160km/h lines, often with modern ETCS signalling and new alignments to increase speeds.

Czech national rail infrastructure manager, Správa železnic (SŽ), has presented plans for the planned VRT network (Vysokorychlostní tratě – high speed lines), which will be built in 13 phases between 2025 and 2050. Until now, no dedicated high-speed infrastructure has been built in the country, although a series of major upgrades, often involving new alignments to remove speed restricted curves, has been undertaken on the main routes from Prague to Olomouc, Plzeň and České Budějovice since 2000.

In 2017, plans were announced to convert all the existing 3kV DC electrification in the Czech Republic to 25kV AC, which will affect 1,796km of the national network route, largely in the north and west of the country.

Illustrating an upgraded existing line, ČD362 060-6 leaves the new 4.15km-long Ejpovice tunnel's western portal at Plzeň-Doubravka, with train Rx774, the 07.03 Praha hl.n to Plzeň, on 17 November 2018. This was the first day of full operation through the southern tunnel; the northern bore did not open until 7 December 2018. (Shaun Wallace)

North-south high-speed corridor
A north to south high-speed corridor is planned from the German border, serving Ústí nad Labem in the north and Brno in the south of the country, with major new through stations serving Prague and Jihlava enroute. This forms the basis for the rest of the network, which would see a branch northwest of Prague serve Chomutov, while two additional high-speed routes will branch east. The first from near Prague would head towards Hradec Králové and then eastwards towards the border with Poland, with the other from Brno east to Ostrava.

Assuming ambitious plans being developed in neighbouring Poland for new high-speed lines come to fruition, new international high-speed connections serving both Wrocław and Katowice may be built long term. As part of the plan, the existing line south of Brno, where a new station south of the city centre is planned, to the Slovak border will be rebuilt for at least 200km/h operation. Test trains have already achieved this speed on the existing line.

The VRT network, which south and east of Prague will be passenger only and designed for 320km/h operation, using 25kV AC electrification and ETCS Level 2 cab signalling, will serve around 5.5 million people, which is roughly half the Czech population. When completed by 2050, 130,000 passengers a day are forecast to use the network. SŽ described its work in 2021 as the 'pre-investment phase' of the entire programme, with construction work on the first sections of the planned network expected to start in 2025.

The 200km/h section from the German border to Ústí nad Labem will be almost entirely in the new 26km-long Krušnohorský Tunnel (11.7km of which is in the Czech Republic) under the Ore Mountains, which form the border. Another tunnel, at least 18km long, will take the new 250km/h line south of Ústí nad Labem under the České středohoří, or Bohemian Central mountains, through which the existing line follows the course of the River Labem (the Elbe in Germany). An intermediate parkway style station near Roudnice nad Labem will be served by domestic trains and connections to other regional towns will be provided.

The entire new route between Prague and Dresden will be mixed traffic, with freight trains also sharing the tracks, mostly at night. Journey times between Prague and Ústí nad Labem will fall from 70 to 25 minutes, with Prague to Dresden taking 51 minutes instead of the current two hours and 16 minutes. The Dresden to Prague line is expected to open around 2035.

ČD 'Railjet', led by 1216 234, passes Vojkovice nad Svratkou, south of Brno, on the 160km/h Břeclav to Brno line, with a Prague to Graz via Vienna service on 1 April 2019. This line will be rebuilt for minimum 200km/h operation.

Planning for the new lines started with strategic assessments undertaken between 2014 and 2018, which confirmed the need for and basic outline of the new routes. The first projects expected to begin construction in the mid-2020s are Prague–Dresden, Prague–Brno–Břeclav, Brno–Přerov–Ostrava, and Praha–Hradec Králové–Polish border.

Construction work is planned to span the period 2025–50 with around 15 billion Czech Crowns (£500 million) being spent every year on construction or planning in that period. The first sections of new railway are forecast to open in 2028. Even longer-term planning is underway for a new tunnel between Praha-Smíchov and Beroun, on the route to Plzeň, but construction is unlikely before the 2030s.

The entire high-speed programme is designed to not only increase rail capacity and speed up journeys, but also to act as an economic stimulant for some parts of the country, enabling better access to employment and other opportunities. The city of Jihlava, which is located close to the planned Prague–Brno route and roughly halfway between the two cities, will see massive improvements in its transport links. Thanks to an out-of-town parkway station planned just east of the town, Jihlava will be 37 minutes from Prague by rail, and under 30 minutes from Brno; current journey times are around three hours to Prague and two hours to Brno!

Initial work to enhance capacity in the Prague area has already commenced, with a new four track section designed for 120km/h replacing an older slower double-track route between Praha Vršovice and Hostivař, in the city's south-eastern suburbs, in December 2020.

Plans for Prague's new high-speed hub, provisionally known as 'Praha Vychod/Prague East', have been developed and the winner of the architectural competition to design the new station was announced in 2021. The planned station will act as a parkway style station, with parking for 3,000 cars.

In mid-2021, the Czech Republic, Germany, and Austria signed an agreement to introduce much faster Berlin–Prague–Vienna trains, when the planned north-south VRT corridor is in place, with four hours and five minutes Berlin to Vienna timings planned. This breaks down as two hours between Berlin and Prague, and two hours five minutes from Prague to Vienna.

The proposed Praha Vychod high-speed station. (Správa železnic)

New trains for higher speed future

While entirely new purpose-built high speed trains will be needed when the 320km/h sections of line open, Czech national operator, ČD, ordered a fleet of 180 Siemens and Škoda Transportation 230km/h coaches in 2021, which will work as 20 nine-coach push-pull sets, enabling faster operation, especially on international routes. In 2018, ČD had already ordered 50 similar coaches to be used for 200km/h loco-hauled services from late 2021. ČD is also planning to obtain more high-speed electric locos able to work with the new passenger coaches.

The 230km/h Siemens/Škoda Transportation push-pull sets ordered in 2021 will have driving vehicles styled like the Siemens 'Vectron' driving cab. (Škoda Transportation)

Upgrades in Slovakia

Slovakia does not have ambitions for a new high-speed network, although significant improvements have been made to journey times through rebuilding sections of the Bratislava to Žilina main line since 2000. In some cases, new sections of line, some involving new tunnels, have been built to replace older slower parts of the route and these are equipped with ETCS Level 2 signalling.

Slovakia is also planning, like the Czech Republic, to convert most of its existing 3kV DC electrification to 25kV AC, this covering the main lines between the Czech border (via Čadca and Púchov) to the Ukrainian border at Chop (via Žilina and Košice).

The Slovak capital, Bratislava, is the eastern end of the Magistrale for Europe, which is an EU-sponsored project aiming to create a high-speed railway all the way from Paris to Bratislava. High speed lines in France (Paris–Strasbourg), Germany (Strasbourg–Munich via new and rebuilt lines from 2025 onwards) and Austria (Wels–Vienna) have already significantly reduced journey times, although currently there are no services from one end of the Magistrale to the other. Austrian Railways (ÖBB) does operate a daily train from Bratislava to Zürich in Switzerland via Vienna.

Conclusions

In 1936, ČSD introduced its two type M290.0 Slovenská strela diesel units and connected Prague with Bratislava in four hours and 18 minutes. By the 2040s, it should be possible to go from Berlin to Vienna via Prague in slightly less time! The changes since 1989 have profoundly altered the railways in both the Czech Republic and Slovakia, with major improvements in comfort and journey times on major routes, while much of the regional and rural rail network remains open, for now at least.

Competition on major routes has undoubtably increased choice and reduced fares, but whether this is sustainable over the long term is unclear. The growth in intermodal and transit freight has led to the Czech Republic, in particular, becoming a key part of the European transport network and has allowed Czech companies to expand into neighbouring countries, such as Germany.

The devolution of rail financing to regional governments tends to work well when government revenues are buoyant, but less so in more difficult times, as seen in Slovakia since 2002, and in neighbouring countries, like Poland, even earlier. The introduction of competitive tendering has reduced operating costs in the Czech Republic, but experience in other countries suggests such savings are largely a one-off, so maintaining the regional passenger network will be an ongoing challenge for politicians and railway operators alike.

Glossary

Place names
In almost all cases, this book uses the current 21st century names for places; where historic names are used, the current equivalent is described as well. The only significant exception is Prague where the English spelling is used in the text, although picture captions use the Czech name Praha when referring to stations or locations.

Railway terms
Nádraží	–	station (Czech)
Železničná stanica	–	railway station (Slovak)
Bratislava hlavná stanica	–	Bratislava main station, abbreviated to hl.st
Praha Hlavní nádraží	–	Prague main station, abbreviated to hl.n
DMU	–	Diesel Multiple Unit
EMU	–	Electric Multiple Unit
VRT	–	Vysokorychlostní tratě (Czech), high speed line

National railway companies
ČSD	–	Československé státní dráhy. The former Czechoslovak national railway company, established in 1918, broken up during World War Two and reconstituted from May 1945 until 31 December 1992.
ČD	–	Českých drah. The Czech state railway and since 1993 the national government owned passenger operator. Renamed České dráhy in 2003 when converted into a company; the abbreviation ČD remaining unchanged. ČD Cargo is the ČD owned freight operator, established in 2007.
SŽDC	–	the Czech national rail infrastructure manager, until 2003 part of ČD. Since 2020, now known as Správa železnic, abbreviated to SŽ. This means 'Railway Administration' and confusingly is also the abbreviation for Slovenian Railways.
ŽSR	–	Železnice Slovenskej republiky. The Slovak state rail railway after 1993 and, since 2002, just the national rail infrastructure manager.
ZSSK	–	Železničná spoločnosť Slovensko. The Slovak national government owned passenger rail operator since 2002. ZSSK Cargo is the freight business, split from the rest of ZSSK in 2005.

Other
Comecon	–	Council for Mutual Economic Assistance, Eastern Bloc pre-1990 trading area.
ČKD	–	Lokomotivka (Českomoravská Kolben-Daněk). Before 1990, it was one of the largest manufacturers of diesel locomotives and trams based in Prague. No longer in business.
Škoda	–	pre-World War Two Czech-based major industrial company, specialising in weapons as well as other heavy engineering. Post-World War Two, the Škoda group built steam, and then electric, locomotives while also making cars. After 1990, Škoda Auto became part of Volkswagen and privatised Škoda Transportation remains a major rail engineering firm.